FOLK LORE

IN

LOWLAND SCOTLAND

FOLK LORE

IN

LOWLAND SCOTLAND

BY

EVE BLANTYRE SIMPSON

NEW ORLEANS
ARABI MANOR
REBEL SATORI PRESS
MMXXI

Printed in the United States & United Kingdom by
Arabi Manor, A Rebel Satori Imprint

Originally published in 1908 by
J. M. Dent & Company,
Bedford Street, London

ISBN: 978-1-60864-186-4

CONTENTS

FOLK LORE IN LOWLAND SCOTLAND

CHAPTER I

BELTANE AND THE VANISHED RACES

> "On the wind-swept moors and tranquil valleys I have felt, by some secret intuition, some overwhelming tremor of the spirit, that here some desperate strife has been waged, some primeval conflict enacted; an uncontrollable throb of insight, that here some desperate stand was made, some barbarous Thermopylæ lost or won."
> —*House of Quiet.*

THE study of the folk lore of Lowland Scotland reveals to us in scanty uncertain glimmers some shadowy conception of the aboriginal inhabitants of what was in sober truth a stern and wild Caledonia. Ancient haunts of men have numberless tongues for those who know how to hear them speak. But it is not the uncouth monoliths like giant mile-stones, looming forth on heights and dark moorlands, but the place names our deluvian ancestors bequeathed to us, which guide us to the knowledge from whence they had wandered to the north. Those that run may not read, but those who pause, and with careful patience clear away the dust of bygone ages, can decipher, despite the obstructions of centuries of progress, traces which, like a blazed trail, lead us beyond the even track of written history into the forest primeval of Scotland's story. Amid all our vaunted complicated civilisation is it not somewhat startling to find we, who consider ourselves so advanced in religious knowledge, adhere to usages descended to us from the sanguinary creed of our blue-woaded ancestors?

One chief and most abiding indication of their, and consequently of our, Oriental origin, are the relics left by these extinct races of their worship of the great lights of heaven. Fire has had a fascination for the human species from time immemorial. Naturally, those who were forced to dwell in the north craved the most for warmth, but whether the blaze is lit by a hearth-stone, or in the open under the roof of heaven, man, civilised or savage, is allured by and gathers round a fire. The glowing flames for the time being become the home centre. In far past ages the inhabitants of Scotland wielded weapons of stone, but later, when the hidden metals had been tracked to their lair, the natives learned to forge bronze swords, the sun, moon, and stars above them were all important mystic factors in their lives—gods to be propitiated. They had to live preying, and being preyed upon by the four-footed people who shared the woods with them. Their roof was a tree, and in winter they sought, like the foxes, shelter in Mother Earth. For all their weather-hardened skins, or robes of deer hide fastened with horn pins, they were a-cold. They looked on the forces of nature as the smiles or frowns of a beneficent or an angered Being. They sought to curry favour with the Power above that gave to them light and heat. From the East they had brought along with them their language, as well as their reverence for Baal. Fire was his earthly symbol, and from his name Baal, Lord, and the Celtic *tein*, fire, comes Beltane — a word which lingers as a beacon light in Scottish place names. Beltane is also linked with our traditional customs, legends, and poetry. To be nearer to their God on the mountain-tops, they built up fires to do him honour. As Solomon says, "It is a blessed thing for the eyes to behold the sun." When the drear-nighted winter was over, the heat of the great orb's rays were doubly welcome. We read in the Old Testament of this worship of Baal, and the manner in which sacrifices of men and beasts were offered to appease or pleasure him. The rites were the same in North Britain as in Tophet, the Valley of Slaughter, when the Lord complained they broke His law. The Druids, those all-powerful priests who swayed the people of this country, appointed certain seasons in which to pay their chiefmost deity homage. These days have remained our national festivals, 1st May, Midsummer, the eve of November, and Yuletide. Besides the white bulls slain in honour of Baal, the Men of the Oaks decreed that a huge wicker cage in the form of a colossal mortal should be woven, and in it were cast a holocaust of human victims. These were not only prisoners, but the worshippers' hearts'-blood, for parents gave their best beloved. Rude music made by striking tightly-stretched hides deadened their dolorous cries. When they had thus paid sanguinary homage to their god, when the lurid flames, lit in his honour, had devoured the giant cageful of their choicest and fairest, the assembled company held high revel, danced and caroused, partaking of peculiarly-prepared food and drink. The foregoing is a brief outline of how the ritual of the sun-worship of the Druids was conducted on the high-placed rude altars on the moorlands, and by others who lived in the old time before them.

We have to surmise much regarding the ways of our ancient ancestors, but the first authentic history of a nation is the history of its tongue. Mountains and rivers still murmur the voices of a people long denationalised or extirpated, so it happens the prehistoric race, who lived in what is now epic Scotland, have left in place names, and also in surviving observances, hints which enable us to grope our way back to embryo eras in our country's chronicle.

The coming of the Romans wrought many changes. They uprooted Druidism, for these conquerors did exactly as was done in the East in King Josiah's time. "They broke in pieces the images, and cut down the groves, and forbade that any man might make his son or daughter pass through the fire to Moloch."

But the old beliefs lingered, though the priests were scattered. Superstition is enduring, especially when mingled with a religious creed. Dr. Jameson mentions that an old Highlander, so lately as the end of the eighteenth century, was in the habit of addressing the Deity under the title of "The Arch Druid." These specified seasons for sacrifices and foul orgies of heathen darkness held by our pagan predecessors are still holidays in this Christian land of ours. When the thorn was white with blossom Merrie England frolicked round the bedecked maypole. In Lowland Scotland, however, the mode and manner of welcoming the spring-time followed more closely customs instituted by those who placed "the grey recumbent tombs of the dead in the desert places; standing stones on the vacant wine-red moor."

Even from ballad history we glean how much in vogue was the keeping of Beltane. The royal poet, James I., pictures for us how, from far and near, the people thronged to the May-day fair at Peebles. This carnival to hail spring was a landmark of time for the lowland Scot even until our own day. The origin of our saying, "Peebles for Pleasure," comes from this spring gathering. James I., in *The King's Quhair*, tells how

> "At Beltane when ilke bodie bownis[1]
> To Peblis to the play.
> To heir the singing and the soundis
> The solace suth to say."

Now in this twentieth century, except for those who rise to wash their faces in the dew on May-day, Beltane has been wellnigh forgotten, even among the shepherds, who kept up this feast and its customs, for only in the latter end of the Victorian era has it fallen into abeyance. Still many scale Arthur's Seat on May-morning, for tradition had so imbued the citizens of Edinburgh with the custom that they yet adhere to it. Even amid the rush of our present-day life, we have to pause, however briefly, to recruit when winter is past and the time of the singing of birds has come. We feel the need of a chance to enjoy the returning strength of the sun, although the old way of keeping Beltane, even among the conservative rustics, has gone, and the religious rest time, "the Preachings," have disappeared. These holydays have been superseded by the more prosaic and scrimp Spring Holiday, a day on which the populace can go forth and see the advent of summer. Mr. Guthrie in his *Old Scottish Customs*, published in 1885, tells how he

[1] bounds.

remembers the manner in which Beltane used to be kept. "The shepherds met ere the dawn of May on some neighbouring heights and round a trench which they cut in a huge ring. They went through certain ceremonies, the formulary of which had been handed down from Baal's votaries. They made a fire of wood, on which they dressed a caudle of eggs, butter, oatmeal, and milk. Each of the company brought, besides the ingredients for making the caudle, plenty of beer and whisky. The rites began by spilling some of the caudle on the ground by way of libation. That done, every one took a cake of oatmeal, upon which were raised knobs, each dedicated to some particular being, the supposed preservers of their flocks and herds, or to some animal, the real destroyer of them. Each person then turned his face to the fire, broke off a knob, and throwing it over his left shoulder, said: 'This I give to thee, preserve thou my horses; this to thee, preserve thou my sheep,' and so on. After this they used the same rites to the noxious animals. 'This I give to thee, O fox; this to thee, O hooded crow; this to thee, O eagle.' When the ceremony was over they dined on the caudle, and after the feast was finished what was left was carefully hidden away by two persons deputed for that purpose, but on the following Sunday the herdsmen reassembled and finished the remains of the former feast." Having gone through many peculiar forms of frolic and mummery, the keepers of Beltane fed and made merry. Then lots were cast by breaking up the oaten cakes and blacking one knob. The drawer of the charcoaled piece from the hat was bound to leap through the blaze three times. Those who, amid the laughter of the onlookers, sprang over the flaring embers with as little scaith as possible would not in times past have escaped with a bound above the burning heat, but have been devoured by the red-tongued flames to propitiate the God of Light. It was also customary at these gatherings for fathers to pass over the fire with their children in their arms to ensure their offspring immunity from ill. Milton touches on the origin of this custom in *Paradise Lost*:—

> "Though for the noise of drums and timbrels loud
> Their children's cries unheard, that passed through the fire
> To his grim idol."

There is a Gaelic proverb which speaks of being in "the jeopardy of Baal." This arose from the practice of lighting two contingent fires and driving those to be sacrificed between them to be consecrated before death. To be between Baal's fire came in local parlance to much the same thing as being between the deep sea and the devil, without hope of escape. The idea of thus purifying the flocks by cleansing fires still dwells with us. In parts of Perthshire in 1810 "the inhabitants collected and kindled a fire by friction, and through the fire thus kindled they drove their cattle in order to protect them against disease." In other parts of Scotland the horses are herded between the two bonfires, thus still unconsciously dedicating them to the sun. Penant, in his *Tour in Scotland*, mentions seeing the hill-tops aglow in honour of Beltane, and Mr. Napier in his book on folk lore, published in 1879, says, "Many think the superstitions of last century died with the century, but this is not so; and as these notions are curious and in many cases important historical factors, I have thought it worth while to jot down what of this folk lore has come under my observation during these last sixty years." He mentions isolated districts where the rural people still held to the observances of Beltane, and talked with those who recollected it when it was more of a national feast day. All fires in Druidical times were quenched on the last night of April. The priests on a neighbouring hill dedicated to the solar worship, from the pyres they lit to welcome May, gave to the people kindling from their sacred beacon wherewith to relight the social watchfires on their own hearths.

Midsummer was the season next set aside to propitiate Baal, but it fell sooner into oblivion than the other specially-appointed feast days. The light was long in June, the sun strong; the flocks fattened on the new luscious grass, for heat and consequently food were plentiful. There was no need to fawn and curry favour with a bountiful patron, so then as now, when all things were going easily and smoothly, man took the benefit as his due and paid small court to the Powers above. A well-known proverb shows the frailty of human beings and the strategy of Satan:—

> "When the devil was ill, the devil a saint would be,
> When the devil was well, devil a saint was he."

The coming harvest caused some anxiety, but Midsummer Day and its never dark night and clear skies did not lend itself to Baal worship. When the summer was over and winter had to be faced, man bethought himself again of courting favour. The exit of October became, and still from custom and tradition's sake remains, a marked day. The Celtic name for this Hallowmass was Sham-in, the fire of Baal. The Irish called it Sain-fuin — sain, summer, and fuin, end—*i.e.*, the end of summer. It was at this season that the Druids usually met in the most central places of their surrounding country and administered justice and adjusted disputes. Those who did not make their peace were not given the brand from the consecrated fire and had a sentence of excommunication passed on them. "Dr. Arthur Mitchell," says an antiquarian, writing in 1867, "informs me that a few years ago he counted within sight of a railway station in Perthshire a dozen of these Samhain fires burning in different directions on a Hallowe'en night. On the eve of the first day of November there were such fires kindled as on May-day, accompanied as they continually were by sacrifices and feastings." The name Hallowe'en for this late autumnal feast in Christian times superseded Samhain. The Romans had a festival called Fernalia in February, when they visited the graves of their friends and offered up oblations. The spirits of the dead were then believed to be free to roam in their whilom earthly haunts, and if not propitiated would, during the ensuing year, haunt their neglectful relatives. Eventually to cloak pagan Samhain with a semblance of Christianity, the Church mingled the two feasts into Hallowmass. On the eve of November it was believed the veil was lifted and a peep into futurity given. Gradually All-Hallow observances were not held on hill-tops, but centred round the people's own fireside, and there nuts were burnt and apples ducked for. Apples have taken root in the superstitions of the people may be from the day of their forbiddenness. A tree of them is said to be lucky near a house, and apples are credited with holding a special sway over the affairs of the affections. One common Hallowe'en custom is for a girl to pare an apple and fling the skin over her shoulder to read from its twists the initial letter of her lover's name. This divination of the future by contortions and signs rose from out of the blood-bestained smoke of Baal's fire. The oak-wreathed Druids learned to draw conclusions as to the future by watching the writhings of their victims, whether bull or man, under their knife, and the way they fell in their dying agony. A less blood-thirsty age reads what is to come in apple skins. From Hallowe'en hankerings for future insight any bold lover had but to be alert, or have a friend to give him a hint when to appear, to score a success. Most of the charms had to be worked out alone, some had to be tested in a solitude of two, which gave a quick-witted youth every opportunity of advancing his suit. There was the pulling of green kail stocks from out of a spinster's or bachelor's garden, when a couple went with shut eyes, hand in hand, among the cabbages. If the runts were of goodly growth, stout of stem, all was well for the pullers. Their mates would be well favoured in person and purse. If the roots were unclogged with earth, they would be lacking in comeliness and poverty-stricken. If the kernel of the stock was sweet or sour to taste, so would be the temper of the future consort. The stocks were hung about the doors, and the next person crossing the threshold was held to bear the name of the future wife or husband. It was thus made easy for a lover to come in at an opportune moment, or to persuade the lady of his choice not to fly in the face of fate, when such opportunities as walking in the dark, with eyes shut, hand in hand, were strewn by tradition in their path. For instance, on this night when the future was seen face to face, maidens ofttimes, while combing their locks, ate an apple alone at midnight, threw one piece over their left shoulder, and while munching the rest, they looked through their veil of hair and saw the reflection of their ordained spouse in the mirror. There is also the old custom of the sowing of hemp. It was also done at midnight by a lass scattering the seed saying, "Hemp seed I sow thee, hemp seed I sow thee; and he that is my true love come behind and harrow thee." A youth who was too faint-hearted to take advantage of such a chance was not worthy to win a fair lady. The winnowing of corn at mirk midnight offered yet another opportunity, also the measuring of the beanstalk. The order in regard to the latter spell was to go three times round a beanstalk with outstretched arms, as if measuring it, and the third time the votary will clasp in her arms the shade of her future partner. It is easy to see how the shadow with a little tact might become substance.

Throwing the clue was another forecast practised. The receipt for this augury was:

"Steal forth alone at night to the nearest lime kiln, and throw in a clue of blue yarn, winding off in a fresh clue, as you come near the edge, grasp hold of the thread lying in the kiln. You then ask who holds, and the name of your future partner will be uttered from beneath." Mr. Guthrie, in his *Old Scottish Customs*, tells us of a girl called Mary Shirley, who had two admirers, Robert Laurie and William Fleming. Laurie was the favoured one. Fleming consulted a friend of Mary's, and found from her that Mary Shirley intended on the coming Hallowe'en to throw the blue clue into the kiln nearest her father's house. Fleming obeyed the hint thus kindly given. On the night in question he hid himself in the lime kiln and seized hold of the clue which the inquiring lass threw in. In answering to her faltering "Who holds?" he gave his own name. Hastily dropping the thread, the terrified girl fled homewards. Ere many hours had elapsed Fleming proposed and was accepted by the pretty Mary, to the no small surprise and anger of his rival. When congratulated on the wisdom of her choice, she replied somewhat sadly: "It was na me who made the choice; I myself was a' for Robert, but fate had it I was tae get the ither, and wha can gang agin fate?" The marriage thus strangely brought about proved a very happy one for both parties. Fleming, however, wisely preserved silence as to the Hallowe'en trick which won him his bride." There were many other observances, all with much the same object, tried with merriment on the eve of November, when people believed the borderland between the visible and invisible world was for a brief space free to dead and living. There was the pricking of an egg, the eating of a herring, the dipping of a shirt-sleeve, etc., each giving golden opportunities to help the prophecy to be realised.

At Rutherglen there long lingered peculiar ceremonies as to the baking of sour cakes on St. Luke's Day. This unique baking was supposed to have originated in pagan times,—the meaning thereof is swallowed up in the darkness of ages. The baking was executed by women who began their work at sunset. They sat within a chalked line, whose bounds were never overstepped by the audience as it was looked upon as consecrated ground. One dame was the toaster or queen, the helpers were her maidens. The dough was prepared beforehand and rolled up into balls mixed with sugar and aniseed. The women's hands never touched the dough; she who sat next the fire towards the east was called the Toddler, her companion on the other side was called the Hoddler, who took a ball, formed it into a small cake and then cast it on the bake-board of the Hoddler, who beat it out a little thinner. This being done, she in her turn threw it on the board of her neighbour, and thus it went round from east to west, in the direction of the sun's course. When it came to the toaster it was as thin as a piece of paper. Sometimes the cake was so emaciated as to be carried by the air up the chimney. The bread thus baked was never originally intended for human food. In later days it was always given to strangers. The origin of this custom is said to be very ancient, and it is thought by some to have belonged to the worship of the moon, for cakes were kneaded by women for the Queen of Heaven. This baking has fallen into abeyance, but for long at Rutherglen sour cakes and salt roasts were prepared for provisions at the time of St. Luke's Fair. Those who are inquisitive as to what had been, can only guess that near to the time of Hallowe'en in pagan times the moon came in for her share of homage. As the spouse of the sun she was held sacred, and Venus was the page to these leading luminaries. The rainbow and the lightning were the sun's servants. Astoreth or Astarte was the name of the moon god, the sun's fair silvery consort, and to this day from ingrained superstition we look for the Lady Moon when she appears but a silver bow in the heavens. For luck's sake we turn our money in our pockets, kiss our hands, or bow to her three times. Job (xxxi. 26) speaks of the worship of this goddess as of some ill religion, the observance of which has descended to us. "If I beheld the sun when it shined or the moon walking in brightness and my heart hath been secretly enticed, or my mouth hath kissed my hand, this also were an iniquity to be punished by the judge for I should have denied the God that is above."

"O Lady Moon—whose horns point to the east,
    Grow be increased.
O Lady Moon—whose horns point to the west,
    Wane be at rest!"

says an olden rhyme. Thus everlastingly fair Lady Moon has been saluted when her silvery horns are first seen. She has waned and gone to rest for untold ages, for millions of moons, and still, till lately, here among us cakes were baked by her woman votaries, still she entices us by her monthly newborn beauty to make obeisance to her. As for the eve of All Souls, the ancient Samhain, when graves give up their dead, and for a space the spirits of good and evil have special licence to return to this world, it will never be forgotten as long as Burns is read, for his imagery of the revel of the witches by Alloway Kirk has made it immortal.

When the days had begun to lengthen the Druids instituted the festival of Yuletide, to hail the slowly-increasing light. The northern nations, like the Hebrews, to use an Irishism, began their day in the evening. They counted time by nights. That was an all-important period, for their sacred fires (which they looked upon as the earthly symbol of the sun) loomed the better against the mirk of the dark hours. The conviviality on the threshold of a new year we still adhere to. In one of our ballads we read of the hallowed days of Yule, for the time of feasting lasted longer than one scrimp day. When people had gathered together from afar, they enjoyed a week or more of social intercourse, as when in James the First's time they "bounded" to "Peebles to the play." Yule and New Year came to be merged as one festival. In Christian times in England, the feast of the Nativity remained the principal holiday, but in Lowland Scotland Hogmanay and the first week of January were the "hallowed days of Yule." Also no doubt owing to the persevering efforts made by the Presbyterian clergy after the Reformation to extinguish all Catholic holydays, Christmas was not regarded north of the Tweed. The last of December, Hogmanay as it was called in Scotland, was looked upon by the children as a period when beggary was justifiable. The foreseeing housewife prepared for the besieging of her door by demanding bairns, and baked Hogmanay cakes. She good-naturedly obeyed the injunctions sung before her house:—

> "Get up, good wife, and shake your feathers,
> Dinna think that we are beggars;
> For we are bairns come out to play,
> Get up and gie's our hogmanay."

In England the people in Christian times learned to sing Christmas carols, but in Scotland, the boys who were guisards sang, or rather hastily, with sing-song voices, gabbled, rhymes, whose meaning is lost in conjecture.

> ". . . Hogmanay,
> Give us of your white bread, and none of your grey."

was one favourite jingle cried by the guisars. To the middle of last century, in outlying primitive districts, at the close of the year, children dressed themselves in sheets, which they folded so as to form an ample pocket like a fishwife's petticoat, to hold their dole. Then they went from door to door, laughing and singing their Yuletide rhymes:—

> "My feet's cauld, my shoon's done,
> Gie's my cakes, and let's rin."

the sheeted blackmailers cried, when they had got their pockets full. Mr. Chambers in his *Popular Rhymes of Scotland*, published in 1841, says: "It is no unpleasing scene (I am sorry to say I speak of sixty years since) to see the children going laden home, each with his large apron bellying out before him, filled full of cakes, perhaps scarcely able to waddle beneath the load. Such a mass of oaten alms is no inconsiderable addition to the comfort of the poor man's household, and tends to make the season still more worthy of its jocund title."

Auguries as to the future were drawn from Yuletide bakings. The farmers' wives in Forfarshire kneaded bannocks at this season. If they fell asunder after being put to the fire, it was an omen that they would not bake again on the eve of Yule. Hansel-Monday followed the New Year, for Scotland has two special holidays of her own—Hogmanay and Hansel-Monday—which she does not share with her southern sister, England. She leaves to the latter Christmas and Boxing Day. Hansel-Monday is the first Monday of the week after New Year, when presents were given in tokens as a symbol of peace and good-will, and Hansel-Monday, as every householder knows, is still a day when those who serve us during the year expect a largesse. In olden times, not only to children and servants were hansels given, but to all the stalled beasts. The farmer went round and laid in each manger an extra feed. Burns alludes to the kindly custom when the master pats his steady steed and says:—

> " A gude New Year I wish thee, Maggie,
> Hae, there's a nip to thy auld baggie."

Every house was set in order and work ceased on Hogmanay. Yarn was hanked and wheel and reel put by. Yule, when the days were brief, was a convenient season to gather round the hearth and burn the Yule log, which was usually of ash.

The holiday was lengthened out in the company of bewitching mead and heather ale, and all the Scandinavians kept the Yuletide by their own hearths. Hogmanay, though seemingly Scotch, is said to be of French derivation from *au gui menez*, "to the mistletoe go," which mummers formerly cried in France at Christmas. Another suggested explanation is *au geux menez*, that is, "bring to the beggars." There are others who hold that Hogmanay comes from a word meaning "the night of slaughter." That derivation of the word recalls the olden days when the cattle were killed in preparation for the feast of Baal. The mistletoe has grown into the flower symbolic of Yuletide. It is a true evergreen, for it reminds us still of the days when the Druids held sway over our pagan land. Whatever be the derivation of Hogmanay, it holds its own in Scotland. Dark men are popular on the dawn of the first of January. The first person to enter a house on the New Year should be black-haired, not a red or fair man, and a woman is unwelcome. Many devices are resorted to to secure a lucky first-foot, so that the house may prosper. The wine of the country is in much requisition on Hogmanay. It is given and taken by the first-foots.

Still in the stubborn Scotch mind, despite centuries of advancement, there remains fixed the idea that the days of Yule should be holiday times. They extend, as in prehistoric years, for wellnigh a week, and there is a pardon given for the noisy carousing on the occasion. Even in this bustling age people find it takes a few days to wish a good New Year to all their friends. The Druids' practice to keep a watch on the night that the old year dies remains with us. Crowds eagerly hearken for the church bells to ring out the old, to ring in the new, and there is not much time given for that "solemn pause" thinking over the year "that's awa'," of which Sir Walter Scott speaks in his journal.

To sum up some of the customs which folk lore from ages past has bequeathed to us, and which, though in a modified form, we unconsciously adhere to, the Druids instilled into their devotees a patriotism which made them strive to die

> " . . . facing fearful odds,
> For the ashes of his fathers and the temples of his Gods."

This habit of self-sacrifice, our recent wars can testify, is not yet extinct. The Druid priests were astrologers of no mean repute; waiting by their altar fires they studied the starry firmament.

From them, as we have mentioned, we learned to calculate time by senights and fortnights instead of by the *days* of the month. They too left us the mistletoe as a plant sacred to Yule. They had gone forth to cut it with the silver knife in their oak groves to lay upon their altar. It is now entwined with holly leaves and is enshrined in our hearths and homes, as a sign that Christmas is near. Their manner of homage reeked with blood, but they gave to their deity their best and most precious lives without stint. "Thine ancient sacrifice a humble and a contrite heart" we have been taught is sufficient offering, but simple sacrifice though it be, we ofttimes let the seasons roll by without tendering it. Standing by some lichen-covered pagan altar we think of the victims, biped and quadruped, who were once slaughtered there to appease the heathen gods, and see that the grass grows green around the spot once saturated with hot life's blood. Yet though Christianity had shone in the land for hundreds of years, the belief that a life given would mollify the powers that be still glimmered among us. Not twenty miles west from the capital of Scotland, my father, Sir James Y. Simpson, to whose genius and benevolence the world owes the blessings derived from the use of chloroform, mentions in one of his archæological essays, " In old pagan times we know that the sacrifice of the ox was common. I have myself often listened to the account given by one near and dear to me who was in early life personally engaged in the offering up and burying of a poor live cow as a sacrifice to the spirit of Murrain." The one " near and dear " was the future doctor's father. The cow was immured at his grandfather's farm, and Sir James's father used to graphically describe to his eager son how he and his brothers propelled the poor victim into its grave, and " I remember," he added, with grisly graphicness, " seeing the earth heaving after the soil was pushed in." This was some time in one of the latter decades of the eighteenth century, and the owner of the cow, Alexander Simpson, of Slackend, farmer and farrier, was a man full of practical common sense. He was so shrewd and pawky it is likely the wretched animal thus buried to allay the plague was on its last legs before it was thus cruelly immured alive; for he also laid aside a corner of a field as an offering to the Evil One—a corner called the Gudeman's croft—and this bit was a stony, useless knowe. The plough left it unbroken, and it was supposed to be appreciated by the so-called Gudeman. Throughout Scotland these "crofts" may be seen.

When a ship is named and launched we speed it on its way, breaking a bottle of red wine over it. This is a relic of that heathen time when great events were baptised with blood. The new vessel on her passage into the sea would have had her way paved with the bodies of prisoners and slaves which she would have juggernauted amid the acclamations of the delighted crowd.

We learned to rear monuments from those far-off ancestors of ours. Those unwieldy stones they raised on bare heights had been placed there with what almost seems superhuman effort, unaided by any mechanical device. They had no roads to drag their memorials along, no tackle to upheave them into their places — these great slabs of rock, which never knew the smoothing influence of a mason's tools. But the people carved upon them incomprehensible circular hieroglyphics which we cannot read. They engraved these pillars of rock with patient labour, for their implements like their monuments were of stone. Our more practical humane age, instead of placing monoliths on high to bear some great name in remembrance, builds with its gold hospitals and schools for the sick and needy. These rugged, be-lichened obelisks with their strange markings were installed in their places amid the sacrifices and shouts of the worshipping heathen. They have withstood the storms of untold centuries, and standing there in their natural, unhewn, rugged grandeur, tell us how we learned to commemorate outstanding deeds and deaths, for from them we were taught to thus write in stone. The names of some of our Scottish hill-tops show to us where our forefathers worshipped, and we read in them our country's story. They are to us rays of light on sun-worship; for instance, Tullie Beltane is the knoll of Baal's fire, and in the statistical account of Scotland, 1848, it is stated that a thick stratum of charcoal was discovered beneath a structure of fine loam on the summit of the hill. When the country people saw it, they expressed no surprise, as the tradition was familiar to them that it was here where the former inhabitants of the country had been in the habit of lighting their Beltane fires. There is a peak in the Cheviots, Yalverton Bell, and these names (for the word Bal or Bell is given to many a knoll), tell where of old the fires were lit, and where the pagans worshipped, and these names telegraph back to us over mighty distances of time significant specimens of the tongue spoken by the first inhabitants of the districts. In the Celtic other names alluding to fire are beacon lights to the archæologist, such as Ard-Andein, the light of the fire; Craig-an-tein, the rock of the fire; Auch-an-tein, the field of the fire. There are besides Stonehenge other remains of pagan temples left in this land; they, too, like the great menhirs of Salisbury Plains, were almanacs in stone. The priests knew by the slant of the sun on its rising or setting what time of the year it was. At Craig-Maddi there are slabs of rock which form a rude altar, one laid table-wise resting on the other two. The name of the Cromlech itself speaks, Craig-Maddi, the rock of God. There, on the solitary moorland, unmistakable history is written, for no one can look at this huge memorial without recognising at once an altar of the hoary past. Greenach in Perthshire, where there is a large stone circle, means field of the sun; Greanchnox means the knoll of the sun. The latter place is now our great seaport on the Clyde, Greenock. There is also Greenan, a river in Perthshire—river of the sun; and there is a Balgreen, meaning the town of the sun. Near to Edinburgh is its harbour, Granton, and in its name is written the fact that ages before Edwin built a burgh on the great rock which had been a Roman fort, and founded high Dunedin, our city of the winds, the Druids had worshipped on this hillock by the sea. The knoll which caught the gleam of the rising or the setting sun is now a villa-laden steep, but here the priests of Baal had stood and watched, and worshipped and walked amid the Stones of Fire centuries before Edinburgh began to emerge from a fortress into a be-castled romance of stone and lime.

Fire was the alarm signal in troubled times, for it sped the news of coming war. The empty braziers on the peel towers of the Borders were once kept charged to be aye ready to be lighted and let their neighbours know that the English had crossed the Tweed. Fire carried the news of the coming of the Armada from south to north with wonderful despatch. The alarm at Plymouth lit the first link in the chain of fire which blazed from hill to hill till "the glare on Skiddaw roused the burghers of Carlisle." Braziers made an effectual line of telegraph in our land. They were in use till last century, for they were used when it was thought Napoleon was likely to invade our isle. The false alarm lit one day made the bold borders make ready with zeal and promptitude. The very bonfires which we light in times of rejoicing are a link with the eras when the sun-worshippers liked to look down from their blazing heights and call, as did the priest whom Elijah challenged on Carmel, "O Baal, hear us." Their love of flames is not extinguished yet in us, their descendants. The gory trace of the sun-cult's fires, like the bloodstains on woodwork, is indelible. We worship a known God, but when we wish to return thanks for blessings received, we toilsomely ascend, laden with burdens of fuel, to conspicuous heights, and there build bonfires and frolic around the flames, pleased that our light should so shine before men; as when every peak from Land's End to John o' Groat's was aglow with our fires of homage to a great Queen, who, victorious and glorious, had ruled over us for sixty years. We rejoiced and made merry, forgetful that, despite the lapse of ages, we adhered to the practice learned by our ancestors from the priests of Baal.

CHAPTER II

THE ROMANS AND WELLS OF WATER

" Regions Caesar never knew
Thy posterity shall sway.
Where his eagles never flew,
None invincible as they."

COWPER.

" The waters murmur of their name,
The woods are peopled with their fame,
The silent pillar lone and gray."

BYRON.

BEFORE the Druids inflamed the people with patriotic zeal to strive against their Roman assailants, traders to our shores had brought Britain into touch with the culture and wisdom of the East, for the adventurous Phœnicians had found in the westmost corner of England there existed a wealth of much coveted metal. Britain was then an all but undiscovered *Ultima Thule* to the civilised world. Herodotus chronicles 500 years B.C. that there was a land beyond the seas called Cassiterides (tin islands). Aristotle expanded this brief note and wrote later: " Beyond the Pillars of Hercules are two islands which are very large—Albion and Ierne called the Britannic, which lie beyond the Celtae." "Here," says Collier, "for the first time in history, we have the number and the names of the islands which form the nucleus of our mighty empire." The Phœnicians concealed the source from whence they drew their supply of tin. Surrounded by her mist-mantled sea, Albion lay screened, so, watchful though the Romans were, for long they failed to find from whence the ships of Tyre and Carthage sailed home laden with their valued cargoes. Spurred by their love of conquest, determined to find and annex the country that was rich in this mineral, the Romans never rested till Julius Cæsar eventually came, saw, and conquered. The persistent, dogged Roman army, which brooked no opposition, forged their iron way with resolute courage past the thin line of civilisation which girded the southern seaboard of Albion, and came, after many years, to the savage, untamed north. They christened the tribes they found there "The people of the woods," and on their maps Scotland became Caledonia. The derivation of the name shows that the country was well timbered, and the invaders repeatedly raised altars to Sylvanus, the god of the woods, for these fanes we still find. There was one where the Leader and the Tweed meet near the village of Newstead, which had been erected by Carrius Domitianus, the prefect of the valiant and victorious twentieth legion. Further down the Tweed there has been revealed a similar votive offering, which forms another instance how much the wild and silvan character of the country disposed the feelings of the Romans to acknowledge the presence of the rural deities. The junction of rivers seemed to be a felicitous spot for such memorials. Where the Teviot mingles with the Tweed there was again an altar to the woodland god. The modern ducal mansion of Floors, looking down on the spot where the second James Stuart came to an untimely end, is close by the site chosen for the shrine erected to propitiate the satyrs and fauns the Romans believed in and with which they peopled the bosky banks and tangled copses of this now romantic district. These altars to the sprites of the greenwood stand near to where, in after time, the great Border abbeys—Melrose, Dryburgh, and Kelso—arose. The fabled flood of Tweed flows for ever and ever through the Merse, seeing as it rolls through the centuries new religions arise, fade, and be succeeded by others. Roman fane and Christian church alike were built, reverenced, and crumbled into dust. Wizards were reared and prophesied by the wide Tweed side, and the greatest of them, Scott, rests by its banks. "Around are the graves of abbots and monks who lived all through Scottish story, heard the tidings of Bannockburn, Flodden, Ancrum, and Pinkie, their matins and their vespers now sunk in one silence of the dead —and only he in the moving creations of William of Deloraine, and Lucy Ashton, and Jeanie Deans has an immortality of memory."

The triple heads of the Eildon Hills, like the unrivalled Tweed at their feet, have witnessed many changes in our land. A modern writer pictures how generations ago our ancestors had climbed to the eastmost peak of the Eildons and there, in the track of the winds, they had built for themselves a village, and raised earthen ramparts around to protect themselves from their foes, human and wolfish. Within the fosse were the wives and children, and the men kept watch over the untamed Merse of Tweed. "One evening the sentinel on the outer rampart looked over an abyss of darkness at his feet, the steep earthwork almost fell perpendicularly to the almost perpendicular hill-side, and in the lull of the wind he heard the hoarse roar of the Tweed, as it swept in flood through the valley a thousand feet below. No light anywhere save the will o' the wisp speaking to his savage heart of bog demons and forest demons, which lured men to untimely graves, or the fires of possibly hostile village forts on the other side of the valley; and behind him lay all he knew of home—the tribe and the chief, his wife and children, his bed of skins and his smoky hut, his favourite dog, and his quiver of flinted shafts. No wonder it was dear and sweet to him, and no doubt he would have gladly spent his last and best blood to save it from demon, beasts, or man, as the Roman who saw on Palatinus the white porch of his home. But one day from the south, somewhere in the vast stretch of forest or fen that lay between them and the Cheviots, their eyes were dazzled by the gleam of sun on bronze armour, and their scouts told them of swarms of swarthy men, of strange speech and grim visage, bearing strange arms and great engines of war through the deep wood, felling the trees, throwing them into marshes, piling stones over them, and moving in a course as straight as a beam of light towards their mountain fastness. What happened to the village fort we can safely guess—a sudden, swift night attack, after a long stealthy climb, and then the short stabbing sword did its work." Though that was an oft-repeated tale on the Roman line of march, the surviving vanquished natives, with hearts anguished for the home and kindred torn from them, fled for shelter beyond the Forth and Tay. These trained legions from the Eternal City thus ousted from their strongholds the denizens of Caledonia's forests. They turned each well-positioned burgh into a fortified camp, every one of which was a rivet in the links of their chain of conquest, another step forward in the path of empire. Empire and road-making went hand in hand, though the tamers of a savage land may have left their handiwork for others to tread on. In this century, many a farm cart lumbering along to some outlying field travels by the Romans' now disused road. Beneath its grass-grown way the stone ground-work tells us it was engineered by those who, over 1500 years ago, were our conquerors. Coaches laden with our kings and queens have driven along their thoroughfares, the very milestones tell how we learned from them to mark distance. It was by the paved streets, which the legions from Italy engineered from Thames to Forth and Clyde, that there travelled to Scotland the message that a new order of things had come into being, which revolutionised the country, and left more mark upon it than all the roads these Romans made, or the fundamental laws they left us. On their eagles' wings to our barbarous, benighted fatherland, there was wafted north the first whisper of the glad tidings of great joy, news that a star of hope and peace had arisen in the East, and its beams would shine and penetrate everlastingly over the world. It was but a vague report at first, that an insignificant few of the Roman soldiery brought with them from the south. The main bulk continued to consult their oracles and rear altars to praise and conciliate the satyrs and fauns whom they believed dwelt in the dark fir forests of Caledonia. Besides discovering this to be so timbered a country that Sylvanus had to be honoured all along Tweed side, the Romans found it bubbling with mineral waters good both to drink and to bathe in. We have to thank our invaders for teaching our ancestors to become votaries of hydropathy, for the conquered people in course of time followed the lead of the masterful men of Italy. Before the Romans came, the original inhabitants of Britain stood in oriental awe of water. From their Eastern ancestors, who had journeyed from sun-smitten plains, there naturally arose an admiring adoration for wells of water, especially for springs bubbling up pure and undefiled from out of the brown earth. Whether the genii of the fountains and rivers were good or evil spirits, our progenitors were uncertain. The water ways of Scotland, now rivers of romance, seemed to them occasionally to be possessed by demons who were hungry for men and beasts. The Borderers realised the perfidiousness of apparently placidly-flowing streams. The honest Tweed, swollen by snow and rain, came thundering through the Merse, sweeping corn and cattle, and all that came within its grasp into its flood. Its neighbour, the brimming Till, meandering with sinuous twists among green pastures, with stealthy patience undermined its banks, and many a man lost his life in its false-flowing waters. In a Border rhyme this sleek, treacherous river was noted for its cannibal propensities:—

> "Says till to Tweed, though you go with speed, and I go slaw,
> For every man you drown I drown twa."

Three lines tell a similar tale of a river further north:—

> "The dowie Dean
> It runs its lean,
> An' every seven years it gets ean."

Rhymes like these, says Alexander Smith in his *Summer in Skye*, "are the truest antiques, the most precious articles of virtu—an authentic bit of terror that agitated human hearts long ago."

It was averred the kelpie (the water sprite) was heard to wail a dirge before it claims a life. Its slogan is one of these sad plaints which the wind pipes, and the waters sing, for nature's voice is often raised as an earnest of woe. Neith was the goddess of inland waters, and she also, our ancestors held, took toll in lives for neglect of propitiatory homage. But the Romans, though believing in water and woodland fetiches, were also learned in medicines. From Africa's northern shores, where in Algeria famed baths exist, to the springs gushing out among the moors and mosses in Caledonia, these keen-eyed Romans discovered and reverenced healing waters. They founded health resorts which are unsuperseded to-day, and round which originally villages, then towns have grown. First the simple spring, upbreaking through the earth, was fenced with stone and mortar, though many a one, which the aboriginal Britons and the soldiers of the south drank from, were forgotten and left neglected. They gurgle on unconfined and unnoticed in solitary contentment, not aggrieved that an unobserving, though civilised people knows them not. The springs whose sanitive qualities were venerated were credited with being under good guidance. In course of time when Christianity spread, pious anchorites, looking for some hermit's cell, settled always beside drinkable water, and so spread around them a saintly peacefulness. Water washed away the dirt of disease, and water, like fire, licking up the fatal microbe which sowed the seeds of death, became a friend to mankind. Fire burnt the plague out of London, and washing in the wells on prescribed days and seasons, without doubt, cured many who in faith had come there to be healed. Fire and water were the joint agents in quelling disease, and worshippers of yore mingled their rights. There were also wishing-wells where people, still induced by grey-bearded superstition, visit. There, resting on some mossy stone near to the eternally flowing spring, they wish a wish and believe the spirit of the water will hear and fulfil it. To obtain benefit from the well, to make a peace-offering to the kelpie who lived near by, the devotees who came to drink steered their course towards the spring, not "withershins" about.

This word (variously spelt, pronounced widdershins) indicates the inbred dislike of our people of going contrary to the greatest of the heavenly lights. Trees in unprotected positions, which in their youngling days have been twisted west to east by the prevailing winds, are said to grow withershins. They are held to be ill-conditioned, or to be possessed of certain uncanny, occult powers. In the *Meeting of the Sun* the author says: "The Llama monk whirls his praying cylinder in the way of the sun, and fears lest a stranger should get at it and turn it contrary, which would take from it all the virtue it had acquired. They also build piles of stone and always pass them on one side and return on the other, so as to make a circuit with the sun. Mahommedans make the circuit of the Caaba in the same way. The ancient dagohas of India and Ceylon were also traversed round in the same way, and the old Irish and Scotch custom is to make all movements deisual or sunwise round houses and graves, and to turn their bodies in this way at the beginning and end of a journey for luck, as well as at weddings and other ceremonies."

In an old song the lady bewails that the Lowlands of Holland have "twined her love" from her. She knew some ill fate would befall her sweetheart when he sailed over "the saut sea," for his ship "went withershins about" on starting. In another ballad the heroine desires her Tommy to bring from the Howe a stick of—

> "Widdershins grow of good rawtree for to carry my tow,
> And a spindle of the same for the twining o't."

Bedevillery was connected with reading sacred words backwards and going the reverse of the sun. Dr. Walter Smith in an early poem speaks of this idea:—

> "Hech! sirs, but we had grand fun,
> Wi' the meickle black deil in the chair,
> And the muckle Bible upside doon
> A'ganging withershins roun and roun,
> And backwards saying the prayer
> About the warlock's grave,
> Withershins ganging roun;
> And kimmer and carline had for licht
> The fat o' a bairn they buried that nicht,
> Unchristen'd beneath the moon."

So those who went to worship at wells took care not to go against the sun, when they brought their sick to drink or wash in the healing stream. At the summit of the Touch Hills, a little to the west of Stirling, there may be seen by the curious a crystal well which in ancient times was believed to possess the peculiar quality of insuring for a twelvemonth the lives of all who drank from its waters before sunrise on the first Sunday of May. In 1840 there were old men and women then alive who in their younger days had been of the number of those who made an annual pilgrimage to St. Corbet's Well on the morning in question. Husbands and wives, lovers with their sweethearts, young and old, grave and gay, crowded the hill-tops in the vicinity of the well, long before dawn, and each party on their arrival took copious draughts of the singularly blessed waters. Another spring in St. Medan's Cave in Wigtonshire had special properties if drunk when the sun rose on the first Sunday of May. It seemed then to be a cure for all disease; and again in Galloway in the parish of Bootle there is a fountain called the Rumbling Well. The sick sat beside it during Saturday night, and drank of it on dawn of Sabbath morning. The water from this well was also taken home in casks, and the believers washed their cows with it, or gave them to drink of these curative waters. The afflicted, who, as the sun-worshippers of old had done, sat waiting for day before they drank of the crystal stream, left humble offerings in return for the good they obtained. The water sprites were not greedy, a little sufficed as a thanks-offering. Ribbons and shreds of garments taken from the pilgrims fluttered on the branches of the bushes and trees that grew near by the spring. Needles and pins were also thrown in, and money sometimes too was left. A coin of the first James Stuart's period was lately discovered beside a fountain in Perthshire. To show how inherent in our nature is the rendering of tribute to the water god, Sir Archibald Geekie, in his *Scottish Reminiscences,* mentions that in a well in Kirkcudbright the lord of the soil told him, in clearing the pool of debris, coins from the days of the early kings of Scotland and those bearing our well-known queen's head of the Victorian era were found. Also he says, seeing a tree gay with colour, for " from a distance it seemed to be decked with blossoms or leaves of black, white, and red," he describes how on nearer inspection they proved to be bits of rag hung up by the pilgrims who had come to drink of the saint's well that gushed forth from the shadow of a tree. When cattle benefited by the water, their shackles and bands were left as a tribute. Madness was cured at St. Fillan's and at some other wells throughout the country. On a pillar at the church of St. Fillan's, supposed to be older than the building in which it stood, the insane were bound and left over-night. If they broke their bonds, it was asserted they were restored to sound mind. Robert Bruce washed in a spring near Ayr, but despite the report that this had cured him, it is feared that he died of leprosy. Water drawn from under a bridge over which the dead were carried, as well as water flowing south, were reputed to possess special powers. In the North of Scotland there is a loch in Strathnaver to which people journeyed to be freed from all manner of diseases. To bring about this happy result they had to walk backward into the water, dip themselves therein, and leave a small coin as an offering. Without looking round, they had to wade in a direct line back to land, and go right away from the loch. St. Andrew's Well in the Island of Lewis was frequently consulted as an oracle when any one was dangerously ill. A wooden tub full of this water was brought to the sick person's room, and a small dish was set floating in it. If it turned sunwise, it was supposed the patient would recover, otherwise he must die. Special fountains proved efficacious when the eyesight was affected, and a draught from a certain loch in the north cured deafness. There is nothing new under the sun. These pilgrims of old, thirsting to partake of purifying waters, were by their trustfulness made whole, like the faith healers of to-day.

Perthshire was peculiarly productive in these Siloams, but all over Scotland wells still called holy exist. Close by Scotland's capital there are many springs whose virtues have been tried. There is St. Bernard's Mineral Well in the valley of the Water of Leith, but it is affirmed on good authority that it was not the abode of a saint of old, but that its medical value was discovered by some of the Heriot School boys in the eighteenth century. Overlooking Edinburgh from the ridge of Liberton Hill is St. Catherine's Balm Well. A thick, oily substance continually floats on its surface. James VI. visited it, and ordered it to be cleared of refuse, properly closed in, and provided with a door and staircase, but thirty years later the wall was destroyed and it was filled up with stones by Cromwell's soldiers. In succeeding reigns it was again restored, and despite the town overspreading to the hill around it, the face of its waters are still sleek with the oily balm which is supposed to be good for those who are afflicted with cutaneous complaints. Another well within ken of Edinburgh is that of Loretto at Musselburgh. The chapel to Our Lady of Loretto was beyond the east gate of the old borough. Pilgrimages from all parts of Scotland were taken to this shrine. Towards the end of the sixteenth century a hermit took up his abode at Loretto who was famed for his miracles. James V. paid a visit to this most noted shrine of Scotland before he sailed to France to woo his bride. The stones from the old chapel were accused of being the first after the Reformation to be devoted to any secular purpose. The people quarried from the chapel to build a jail. For this piece of sacrilege the inhabitants of Musselburgh were annually excommunicated at Rome, till the end of the eighteenth century.

Within nearer range of Edinburgh, under the shadow of Samson's Ribs, there are the Wells of Wearie. Their romantic, alliterative title has caught the ear of poets. In an old ballad one sings:—

" And ye maun gang wi' me, my winsome Mary Grieve,
There is naught in the world to fear ye;
For I have asked your minnie and she has gi'en ye leave
To gang to the Wells o' Wearie.

O! the sun winna blink in your bonnie blue e'en,
Nor tinge your white brow, my dearie;
For I will shade a bower wi' rashes long and green
By the lanesome Wells o' Wearie."

Another, who was recently well named the Benjamin of Edinburgh's gifted literary sons, in his *Songs of Travel* says:—

" She rested by the broken brook,
She drank of Wearie Well,
She moved beyond my lingering look
Ah, whither none can tell."

How these springs at the feet of the great, green, lion-shaped hill, which keeps everlasting watch and ward over Edinburgh, came by its name, we know not. It may have been a rest-and-be-thankful nook where the tired wayfarer would pause and wash away travel-stains before entering the be-castled grey town.

Throughout the length and breadth of Scotland there are preserved wells still visited and cared for, because they are credited with healing powers, for custom has become part of our inheritance, and they, since the days of the far-off past, have been held sacred. There is a well of as clear water as ever sparkled, by the trout-famed river Whitadder, where it ripples past Abbey St. Bathan's in Berwickshire. It was a shrine for pilgrims, for a road leading to it, still named the Pilgrim's Path, is kept swept and garnished. It runs parallel to the Bishop's Walk in the same precincts. The votaries who hied to St. Bathan's Well quaffed honest water. The many anchorites who in course of time became saints, seeking secluded spots wherein to lead their solitary, religious life, always settled by some fountain. The monks from the neighbouring monasteries, to glorify the example of their lonely brethren, made pilgrimages to these hermitages, and spread over the springs near the recluses' cells an odour of sanctity. The people, doubtless from more heathen ages, had paid court to water and readily followed the footsteps of the holy men. Their idolatry must have savoured of heathenism, for as early as 1182 Anselm banned well-worship, and in 1638 the General Assembly of Scotland waged a determined warfare against it and other relics of barbarian observances however cloaked by religion. "If persons were found superstitiously," states the law, "to have passed in pilgrimage to Christ's Well, near Doune, Perthshire, on the first Sunday of May, to seek their health, they shall repent in sacco (sackcloth) and linen three several sabbaths, and pay twenty pounds Scots for ilk fault." This shows how superstition and religious beliefs are mingled; they are wellnigh impossible to eradicate, especially from the Celtic mind, which is particularly retentive of tradition. Pope Gregory (he who sent missionaries first to this pagan land, for legend reports that he, seeing in the slave-market of Rome some golden-haired Northumbrian children, would not have them named Angles but angels) ordered his missionaries not to thwart the people altogether in their long-implanted heathen habits. Augustine, one of his messengers to this country in the sixth century, was instructed to bear in mind that the pagan temples were not to be destroyed, but turned into Christian churches, that the oxen slaughtered for sacrifice should still be killed with rejoicings, but their bodies given to the poor, and that the refreshment-booths round the heathen temples should be allowed to remain as places of jollity and amusement for the people on Christian festivals. He realised, with diplomatic tact, that it is impossible to cut abruptly from hard and rough minds all old habits and customs, for he who wishes to reach the highest place must rise by steps and not by jumps. These wily measures taken to gather the pagans about their Christianised fanes were, however, two hundred years after the Romans had returned to Italy. A modern writer says of these southern subjugators of ours, " a few military roads and doubtful sights of camps and towns, a few traces of public works, all indicating a despotic military occupation of the country and none of a civilised condition of the mass of the inhabitants, alone remains to tell the world that here the Roman power flourished for four hundred years." But we must remember we also owe them a debt of gratitude that some among their legions carried to these then far-off islands the rudimentary report of the gospel of Christianity, as well as their initial lessons in laws and in medicines which they taught us. Modern science, with its manifold discoveries of material that can be yoked to work for man's welfare, was, after all, not so far ahead of these far-seeing Romans. Radium is found by their mineral wells. Our invaders in days of old, of course, knew not of it, but in this then wild, untutored country they found among the forests and fens these health-giving springs whose waters possessed strange healing powers. Round them they built their villas, and settled as much as ever they settled in this their northernmost province, the last they annexed, the first they abandoned. They came here but on an errand. They fulfilled their task, then returned, for their hearts were in Italy. They certainly made the best they could of this mist-shrouded isle when duty stationed them here, and from them our ancestors learned the rudiments of hygienics. They buried without the walls of their towns, laying their dead oftentimes round some pagan fane, but they took care that the temple was beyond their city's gates. When in course of time churches were scattered throughout the land, people wished to place the mortal remains of those who had gone hence under the shadow of the church, so Roman hygienics were forgotten, and it might have been well for the health of the living community if in this rule they had adhered to Roman law. The first authorised medical officers in our isles came with the Roman legions.

They brought with them doctors to attend their troops. The marshes and woods of Caledonia were far more destructive to the Roman invaders than were the spears, long swords, and scythed chariots of its painted and almost naked warriors. The following was an order of the Emperor Aurelian, 270 A.D. "Let each soldier aid and help his fellow, let them be cured gratuitously by the physicians, let them give nothing to soothsayers, let them conduct themselves in their hospitia, and he who would raise strife, let him be lashed." There are Roman monuments raised in Britain to physicians who died in service. One lived but twenty-five years, and the stone and its inscription found in Northumberland is preserved at Newcastle Museum.

The Romans left their indent on our folk lore, and taught us to hold springs sacred. Science has trained us how to benefit from the mineral wells. Endless centuries of approaching them *not* withershins about has become as a second nature to us, for we deal cards and pass the bottle round deisual or sunwise. In parts of our native land, when the dead are laid in their graves, their resting-place is approached by going round in the same manner. The bride is conducted to her future husband in the presence of the minister round the company east to west on the south side.

Among the endless magical and medical properties that were formerly supposed to be possessed by human saliva, one is almost universally credited by the Scottish schoolboy up to the present hour, for few of them ever assume the temporary character of pugilists without duly spitting into their hands ere they close their fists; as if they retained a full reliance on the magical power of the saliva to increase the strength of the impending blow, if not to avert any feeling of malice produced by it—as was enunciated eighteen centuries ago, by one of the most laborious and esteemed writers of that age.

Pliny thus alluded to, in his *Natural History*, xxviii. 7, says, "Some persons also before making an effort spit into the hand in the manner above stated in order to make the blow *more* heavy."

Many Roman marriage customs remain amongst us—such as carrying the bride over the threshold of her new home and the objection to marriages in May, for that month was dedicated by the Romans to propitiate the spirits of their dead. During that moon their temples were shut, and further, "for any couple to contract marriage during this season was held to be a daring of the Fates which few were hardy enough to venture." Ovid speaks of the ill luck of lighting Hymen's torch in May.

June, called after the wife of Jupiter, to make amends for the banning of the previous thirty-one days, smiled on marriage, and her name month was considered a lucky time to be espoused in. Though

"Like the swell of some sweet tune,
May glides onward into June,"

so strongly ingrained is the Roman custom still, that it has become universal in all classes not to marry in May. How widespread is this belief the smallness of the marriage column in the *Scotsman* proves. Many other oddments of the Romans' residence here remain distinctly visible in our own time. Among others is the *Corydalis lutea*, one of the fumitories, which is a native of the Campagna. It grows on the Borderland on the Roman wall. To this small "short-lived star of earth" some lines are addressed to-day by Sir George Douglas, while musing there on Hadrian's dyke:—

"Thy bloom the scent of honey yields,
And thou with spring dost blow;
A Roman flower in English fields
As bright as long ago!

Till as one dreams and idly thinks
On wars and conquests vain;
A simple pastoral garland links
Earth's mightiest nations twain."

Likely the ancestor of this floweret some soldier of the south brought with him—a keepsake from his sweetheart. Warmed and ripened on his heart, when he fell it took root in the cold northern land and flourished despite the unkindly climate. The little alien fumitory is typical of folk lore, Roman or otherwise. It refuses to be eradicated, and shines forth along our twentieth-century paths, telling those who care to look of the conquering race who held us once in thrall.

CHAPTER III

THE SCANDINAVIANS

> ". . . from Fife,
> Where the Norwegian banners flout the sky."
>
> SHAKESPEARE.

> "When Denmark's raven soared on high
> Triumphant through Northumbria's sky,
> And the broad shadow of her wing
> Blackened each cataract and spring."
>
> SCOTT.

THE Phœnician tin-seekers and the Roman conquerors brought to Britain, as we have seen, new ideas and new beliefs, besides endowing us with new resources by opening up the hidden treasures of the mines. Each race as they came to trade or subject stamped traces of their residence on our folk lore, but it was undoubtedly the Scandinavians who left most impress on our character and customs. Their raven flag succeeded the all-conquering Roman eagle. The ensign bearing the king of birds had soared over Britain from the time the nameless Roman standard-bearer of the tenth legion, on their first approach to the strand, had earned deathless renown by leaping into the surf crying, "Follow me," and the hesitating warriors followed their flag. From that time for some four hundred years the Romans ruled us, but when our southern conquerors followed their eagle back to its eerie in the Eternal City, in this northernmost *Ultima Thule* of their sword-acquired lands, the natives were gathering themselves together to grow into the world-possessing power the Druid sage had foretold would be Britain's destiny.

> "Rome shall perish—write that word
> In the blood that she has spilt;
> Perish, hopeless and abhorr'd,
> Deep in ruin as in guilt.
>
> Then the progeny that springs
> From the forests of our land,
> Arm'd with thunder, clad with wings,
> Shall a wider world command."

At that period a seemingly ill wind blew to our shores pillaging bands who in the end wrought this nation lasting good. As Mr. S. Laing explains in his *Kings of Norway*: "All would have been Roman in Europe to-day in principle and social arrangement—Europe would have been like Turkey, one vast den of slaves, with a few rows in its amphitheatre of kings, nobles, and churchmen raised above the dark mass of humanity beneath them, if three boats from the north of the Elbe had not landed at Ebbsfleet in the Isle of Thanet fourteen hundred years ago, and been followed by a succession of similar boat expeditions of the same people marauding, conquering, and settling during six hundred years, viz., from 449 to 1066. All that men hope for of good government and future improvement in their physical and moral condition—all that civilised men enjoy at this day of civil, religious, and political liberty, the British constitution, representative literature, the trial by jury, security of property, freedom of mind and person, the influence of public opinion over the conduct of public affairs, the Reformation, the liberty of the press, the spirit of the age—all that is or has been of value to man in modern times as a member of society, either in Europe or in the New World may be traced to the spark left burning on our shores by these northern barbarians. The same seed was no doubt sown by the old Anglo-Saxons and by the Northmen, for they were originally the same people; but the seed of the former had perished under Roman superstition and church influence during five centuries in which the mind and property in every country were subjugated to the priesthood whose home was at Rome; and the seed of the latter flourished, because it was fresh from a land in which all were proprietors with interests at stake, and accustomed, although in a very rude and violent way, to take a part, by Things or assemblies of the people, in all the acts of their government."

It was well for us that the wind of God—the nor'-easter — encouraged these sea pirates to come "conquering from the eastward." "Lords by land and sea," they made a happy hunting-ground of our coasts, and owing to their blood we inherit that goodly heritage, the mastery of the ocean. They imbued us with an undying love for "the beauty and mystery of the ships and the magic of the sea," till—

> "Never was isle so little, never was sea so lone,
> But over the sand and the palm trees an English flag has flown."

These strong-handed, strong-willed Norsemen needed no laboriously-made road for their armed men to traverse. Their highway was across a field of foam, and with their sailor-trained, keen eyes and shrewd wits they judged from their galleys what manner of country they had reached and where the richest spoil lay. Ofttimes the poor Britons must have been terror-stricken when they saw the sails of these dare-devil Berserkers looming in the distance. They were a race who loved to look on the bright face of danger, to whom the scent of blood was sweet, and the clang of arms in battle intoxicating music. Possessed of a robust strength, and capable of accomplishing incredible exploits, they came and settled where they listed. They brought with them, not the culture and sins and civilisation of the Romans, but that glory in seafaring, that unquenchable thirst for world-wandering which, united to a grim courage, a love of enterprise and of freedom, has helped to weld Britain into an Imperial dominion. The legends and customs which are our use and wont to-day they brought with them. They dwelt with that wide thoroughfare, the German Ocean, for ever lapping or surging at their very doors, and also as if to spur them to ride thereon "with horse of tree"; above their homes, their veritable roof trees, there towered the Norway pines, each worthy to be "the mast of some great ammiral." Thus, their spirit of adventure egging them on, with timber ready to hand, they turned naturally to shipbuilding. They wielded the axe and hammer with a will, for their hands longed to handle the oar. The necessity of foraging for food also drove them afield, for as Conan Doyle truly says, "Cold and poverty and storm are the nurses of the qualities which make for empire." The hardy Norsemen could not rest satisfied with steadily and bucolicly tilling their stationary corner of ground. Their instincts led them to plough the waves, and their brains were the brighter by reason of their wanderings. The Norsemen, when winter and rough weather held them captive, sat round their fires and recited tales of their own or their forefathers' doughty deeds. The chiefmost theme, however, were legends of Odin and his strong sons. Truly giants walked on the earth in their days, and the stories of their prowess did not diminish in the telling, indeed they grew in stature as time rolled on. "Far-away fowls have fine feathers" we know, and there is an equivalent Gaelic proverb which avers, "There are long horns on cattle in mist." These Northern heroes and the beings and monsters who figure in their myths grew bigger and bigger as the dark of ages enshrouded them. Their human prototypes had doubtless been splendid fellows. They came of a race whose portion and lot were likened to that of the younger brother of fairy story, who was compelled by ill-usage to go forth to seek his fortune. He went out into the world and worked—the elder brother stayed at home in slothful ease, in the slumberous air of the luxuriant East. The younger brother, strengthened with his trials and struggles, eventually grew into a renowned man. Honest of purpose, yet observant, he cleared away all difficulties which obstructed his path, and by his caution and cleverness he acquired wealth and received visible rewards. The younger brother's portion was the Scandinavians' and ours. His descendants carry on the tradition he left. From generation to generation they leave home to seek or improve their fortune. It is they who with a will take up the white man's burden and obey the injunction:—

> "In patience to abide,
> To veil the threat of terror
> And check the show of pride;
> By open speech and simple,
> An hundred times made plain,
> To seek another's profit
> And work another's gain."

Besides fighting the savage wars for peace, they

fight with the forest, and if it by its deep-rooted obdureness does not frustrate their efforts and feed on their bones, they extend civilisation and cultivate lands which have remained untilled since the creation. The Romans left us the ruins of altars to Sylvanus, their wood god. The Norsemen, with their axes and their stubborn courage, taught us how to clear away the impeding trees and turn what had once been primeval wood into fertile fields. It is these intrepid-spirited younger brothers of ours who to-day continue to extend the empire and defend its furthest outpost. They do not forget the—

> " Grey old weary mother
> Throned amid the Northern waters,"

but return again to her rich in this world's gear by reason of their perseverance, having used their talents with energy and wisdom. It is the younger brother who, when he has set his affairs in order, visits his opulent but indolent elder brother whose heritage is waning by reason of his despotic greed. It is he who " fills full the mouth of famine," and institutes law, order, freedom, and education in the neglected dominion, as for instance Britain, the younger brother of to-day, has turned his attention to India, the rich, lazy, effete elder.

On our folk lore as on our character, the Norse left a deep indent. One, writing of the Northland and its battle-loving sea-rovers, who took long to adopt, or adapt themselves to, the gentle tenets of Christianity, says: "It is not surprising that there, rather than in any other part of Europe, we should find the old world wants, and hopes, and fears, dark guesses, crude imaginings, child-like poetic expressions, crystalised into a pretty definite system of belief and worship. We can walk through the glittering ice halls of the old frozen faith, and count its gems and wonder at its fearful images; but the warm heart reachings from which they alike flowed, we can only darkly feel at best, and narrowly pry into here and there."

The barbarian Northmen formed out of their myths a healthy-toned worship of their own. Odin was their all-powerful ideal of a god-like man whose word was law. He ruled over Asgard, the stronghold he had created, throned on its heights among nebulous clouds. In it were Norns who spun perpetually the web which formed the destinies of men. They were the

Fates, giants' daughters, the avengers of wrong. Odin dwelt truly under a roof tree for the great ash, the Yggdrasil, spread its branches over him. The editor of Mallet's *Northern Antiquities* says: " We are inclined to regard this mythic tree as the symbol of ever-enduring time, or rather of universal nature ever varying in its aspects, but subsisting throughout eternity. It is called somewhere " Time's hoary nurse," and we see the principles of destruction and renovation acting upon it." We annually welcome two offshoots of Odin's ash among us, for the Christmas tree and the gaily-bedecked Maypole are both saplings from this giant stem. From Asgard, where its stalwart heroes used to take walks abroad just to see if any entertaining adventure would befall them, we gather many of our legends and myths. The Northmen, who were so long in adopting Christianity, we conjecture from folk lore had, out of their romantic tales, concocted a scheme which accounted for the manner in which this earth's machinery moved. They also formed ideas in regard to their future state which had a ring of reasonable soundness in them. These sea-born ancestors of ours were gifted with forethought and judgment. Of course their scientific knowledge was centuries behind the times, but the practicalness and poetry in their theories and ideas comes into view when we read of the punishments meted out by Odin to the idle dwarfs and elves, which resulted in the ultimate benefit of mankind, for the ill-doing dwarfs were sentenced to toil in the darksome under-world to give to those above fuel and gems, and the light-fingered elves were taught to assist the sunshine and the showers in unfolding the secrets long wrapped in the sheltering snows of winter. Legend made Odin into a just, benign All Father, whose bravery and nobleness was an example worthy of worship. A fire-eater in these days was the only august personage, and Odin was great both as a warrior and as a ruler. The Norseman's heaven was a place full of men who had fought a good fight, taking their ease after war. They had a hell, one might almost say in these complacent advanced days, of the old-fashioned sort. It was a burning spot in the centre of the earth, and the dwarfs pressed to work for the good of the community were its stokers. Odin was a nobler, more practical deity than the gods the civilised Romans had bowed down to. Odin's followers in their downright, direct manner, from their mythical legends, forged and hammered out for themselves a high standard to attain in this life and a belief in the world to come. Their gods were deified men with aims and objects of human interest, masterful, noble giants, towering above other mortals by reason of their strength and force of character, triumphant conquerors in every fight. In those days when a strong sword was the best and only charter needed to claim land and honours, a mighty man was the now humble smith. The Norseman believing that to be slain in battle, or to deal a deadly wound to an enemy was a passport to the halls of Odin, was careful to take with him when he went hence his sword and spear, along with his smith's tools wherewith to sharpen his treasured weapons. He fashioned shield and buckler with all the skill he could, for he looked on them as his eternal companions. As tools of war were so all important centuries after the followers of Odin had been resting in Valhalla, the trade and skill of the smith was held in esteem. Odin, according to legend, wrought at the forge to make for himself flawless weapons worthy of his prowess. His horse Sleipnir, whose careering flight was likened to the swish of the wind rushing at terrific, unimpeded pace along, was shod by Odin's own hand, and perhaps owing to the reverence in which his steed was held, the shoe which it may have cast in its unsurpassed career was treasured, so horse-shoes to-day are held to bring good fortune to their finder. These Scandinavians bequeathed to us many a story, and named us many a name. Day after day as the weeks run round, we have obtruded on our notice the deities who were worshipped by our sea-loving forefathers. The Druids gave us the fashion of recording time by nights; the Scandinavians have named for us the days of the week, and so as we count the fleeting hours we keep in remembrance our pagan, pirate progenitors. Sunday may bulk largely as the first of the seven. It is to us "the quiet hollow scooped out of the windy hill of the week" as George Macdonald calls it; but to the Norsemen Wednesday must have been all important, for it was named after Odin, commonly called Wodin. The old spelling is shown in the well-known ballad of Sir Patrick Spens:—

> "We hoised our sails on a Moneday morn,
> With all the speed we may;
> And we hae landed in Norroway
> Upon a Wodnesday."

Wodin's day came shortly after Sun and Moon days, but between Odin's twenty-four hours and those sacred to the Queen of Night came Tyr's day. Odin's thunderous son, he whose strong hammer sent sparks from the cloud, the powerful Thor follows Wodin in our calendar, and after him came Freya's day. The last twenty-four hours of the week were dedicated to Sætern. Besides these names in daily use the Northmen christened many a spot around our shores. Places easy to them of access became their headquarters. In winter when, owing to the smallness of their boats, they rested from their life on the ocean, they settled themselves on islands as being both secure and convenient, as there were many paths across the sea whereby to leave if a stronger force came. The Islands of the Hebrides bear trace of their residence in the names they gave them, for among the Celtic nomenclature there are many Scandinavian o's and ay's, for instance, eight Fladdas—*i.e.*, flat isles, three Scalpas—ship's isles, some Pabays—priest (father) isle, and Raasay—roe isle.

The monasteries and nunneries which were near to the North Sea fared badly at the hands of the Scandinavian pirates. Even the Cross did not awe them. King Olaf Trgyvason, the "beautifullest man ever seen," went over Norway "with a rough harrow of conversion" as Carlyle explained; but the Northmen had travelled down the ages far from Odin's creed, and along with their valour and robust strength they were deemed to be in no-wise unmanly, despite a vein of avarice and cruelty which made them steer towards the spoils of the Church, and not only men but women and children suffered from their blades, for such were the ethics of their day. They swept out of the Outer Isles much material trace of the mission of St. Columba.

It was round their winter fire when inactive, owing to the season, that the tales of stirring deeds were told in these isles to keep green the memory of the men "great in song craft and hands that loved the oar." The fame of these heroes descended by word of mouth till collected about the time the Normans invaded England by Sæmund the Learned and others, and became known as the Edda. There is the poetic or Elder Edda full of the mythological tale of the birth of the world and the adventures of the gods, which was the golden age of the Northmen, but "the golden age ceased when gold was invented."

The yellow metal became as an apple of discord among them, and the god-like heroes, seized with a lust for the acquiring of gold, quarrelled. The Skalds speak of the gold as feminine, " a worker of evil magic arts she knew and practised. Ever was she the joy of evil people." From one of these sagas we have an idea of the kind of life led by these heroes of Asgard. They for ever sailed westward. " Where shall we go ? " asked Odin when he and his kinsmen looked for new worlds to conquer and settle in. " Southward," he explained, " heat lies, and northward, night. From the dim east the sun begins his journey westward home." " *Westward home*," shouted they all, and westward they went. The name of their great saga, the Heimskringla (the world's circle) was a true one, " conquering from the eastward they circled the globe." They settled in small, determined bands on our shores and took what they listed. They were not averse as time went on to turn their swords into ploughshares, though they were ever readier to handle the former. The men of the woods and wilds held that the plough was an enemy, and so it was to a hunting community. In northern lore there is always a hatred to peace and its civilisation, and the driving away of that spoil which falls captive to bow and spear. The fairy arrows were always directed at the ploughman to scare him from his work. The Boer to-day resents the farmer growing crops and cultivating the veldt.

The Norsemen and the Anglo-Saxon (both sprung from the same stock) came here in the days before the world was waxen old. They were alike descendants of the "younger brother" who went out and did. We owe much to them. They inoculated us with a desire to assume the sceptre of the sea—a nation "whose merchants are princes, whose traffickers are the honourable of the earth." They laid the foundations of our Parliament. They had for their conclaves the green mound with its grassy steps for the speakers and hearers to stand or sit on. Tynwald Hill still hears the Manxman issue laws in that little kingdom in the centre of the British Isles. The name of this "Thing" wald is in our place names in Scotland. Like the stone of destiny the law-makers have journeyed off to the banks of the Thames; there, enclosed with walls and state, no longer, as in Asgard, with the "blue dome's measureless content" for a roof tree, they hold their conclaves.

The Norsemen were no architects. "The name of the main body of the Gothic church—the nave, naves or *ship* of the building—is the inside of a ship turned upside down and raised on pillars," but this word nave, suggestive of vaulted aisles, is all their contribution to our architecture. The axe was a familiar tool in their hands, and they wielded a hammer with the skill descended from Thor, so they made their houses as they did their ships of wood, and thatched them with rushes from the lake. Wood did not withstand the inroads of time. They left no sign of their whilom homes as did the burrowing Picts with the cunningly-narrow entrance which one man could guard. The Roman villas with their inlaid floors are laid bare to-day, but of the Scandinavians' homes we have no trace, though in their last resting-places we have still with us a trace of their handiwork. Their "grave goods" dug from the grassy barrows of the happier dead, where they laid their chief slain after battle, are in our museums, for they buried their dead with their clothes fastened by brooches which have survived. On the Fife shores of Tay was a field called locally the field of the Danes' gold. Digging there lately men of Victoria's era came on golden ornaments richly wrought in the precious metal. That same Fife, from its being a peninsula, was a spot overrun by the piratical Vikings, so it is not astonishing there was found there recently a man all in shining armour clad, buried in a knowe by the present roadside. Local folk lore dubbed the mound Norrie's Law. This armed man of old had struck terror into bygone Fifers with that self-same sword, and in that kingly suit of armour defied their blows. When death claimed him, his followers buried him in the silver mail and he—

> " . . . whose gallant deeds
> Haply at many a solemn festival
> The skald hath sung,"

with his prized blade rusted, his bones dust, in the Victorian era was robbed of his long-preserved grave goods by the folk of Fife.

Though the Scandinavians left us no cathedrals to show their handiwork, the tales told by their hearths survive. In the long nights of winter, when anchored on land, within their wooden homes by their firesides, or at the banqueting board, skalds sang of their skippers' conquests in the summer, and of the prowess of the heroes long gone hence. So the history descended to us—

> " . . . of the sea fight far away
> How it thundered over the tide."

The Norsemen gloried to hear of the doughty deeds when winter and rough weather held them captive, and the time soon came when these oral tales of eld were written down. "A nation's literature is its breath of life, without which a nation has no existence—is but a congregation of individuals." The tales of the sea-kings make the heart of this nation still throb. During the five centuries in which the Northmen were riding over the waves and conquering wheresoever they landed, the literature of the people they overcame was locked up in a dead language and within the walls of monasteries. But the Northmen had a literature of their own, rude as it was.

Nowadays, with paper so attainable every child can get a book to scribble in, we forget at the time when the Normans were going to cross the silver streak and invade South Britain, that not only was a knowledge of writing needed to transcribe the sagas, but material on which to write. Parchment was rare; fair skin, dark skin, and wrinkled skin are names applied by Torfæus describing parchment to his correspondent at Copenhagen, and to get parchment enough to inscribe a chronicle thereon meant money. The very derivation of the word book carries us back to the time when, as Collier in the opening page of his English literature describes how, in "the depth of some Asiatic forest shadowy with the green fans and sword blades of the palm tribe, a sinewy savage stood one day long ago etching with a thorn on the thick fleshed leaf, torn from the luxuriant shrub wood around him, rude images of the beasts he hunted or the arrows he shot—the first step was taken towards the making of a book. Countless have been the onward steps since then, but the old fact that the tree is the parent of the book still survives in many well-known words. For example, take the Latin *liber* and the English *book* and *leaf.* Who does not know that *liber* means originally the inner bark of a tree. Book is merely a disguised form of the word *beech,* into which it easily changes when we tone down *k* to *ch* soft. The word leaf tells its own tale." Even with centuries of progress it took Torfæus time and money to get his various complexioned parchments sent to Iceland. It seems to us even nowadays a far-away spot, and strange that books should have emanated from there when written deeds were scarce, but we must remember from bare isles all that was good and cultured came. Iona sent us Christianity. From Lindisfarne, before its great church on the sandy islet was reared in stone, the monks made the most beautifully illuminated Bible, which is still to be seen, though the Priory's roofless aisles are crumbling. Iceland was formed by a colony of strong, intelligent men who had emigrated from Norway to avoid some tyrannical laws of Harold Haarfager's. "New England perhaps and Iceland are the only modern colonies ever founded on principle and peopled at first from higher motives than want or gain; and we see at this day a lingering spark in each of a higher mind than in populations which have set out from a lower level. The original settlers in Iceland carried with them whatever there was of civilisation or intelligence in Norway; and for some generations at least were free from the internal feuds, and always were free from the external wars and depredations on their coasts which kept other countries in a state of barbarism." So from the strange, ice-girt island with its volcanic fires laying it waste, there has been given us a written chronicle of these tales told in the Sea-kings' hall. We follow in black and white the deeds of valour done so long ago, and learn from this parchment history how these Northmen left us not only the birthright of their blood, but also laws and customs which are ours to-day, and also bequeathed to us legends and myths telling of the time when:—

> "There dwelt men merry hearted
> In hope exceeding great;
> Meeting the good days and the evil
> As they came in the way of fate."

CHAPTER IV

FAIRIES

> " Up the airy mountain
> Down the rushy glen,
> We daren't go a hunting
> For fear of little men,
> Wee folk, good folk,
> Trooping all together,
> Green jacket, red cap
> And white owl's feather."
>
> WM. ALLINGHAM.

GIPSIES, to the novelist, have proved themselves invaluable allies, helping them to work the machinery of their plots by guiding heroes successfully through woods or wastes, protecting them from robbers, and extracting them from seemingly impregnable prisons. To the teller of tales by the fireside the fairies take the gipsies' place, and become the helpers and unravellers of the webs the fates have woven round the central figures of their story. The fairies in the annals of folk lore are a host in themselves. They have remained pre-eminent in the popular creed for centuries, and as Sir Walter Scott says: " They are a most pleasing legacy of fancy." The giants who walked the earth in days of old, as centuries rolled on grew too monstrous to associate with human beings, but their antitheses, the fairies, obtained an entrance into people's hearts and homes long lingered, nay, still remain there, welcome guests, for there is no doubt that the fairies who won their way deep into the affections of mortals, and had a seat by every hearthstone when the world was young, still dwell with us. They have been the companions and delight of countless generations of children. Fairy lore and its moral teaching has remained indelibly fixed on their memories from youth to second childhood. Giants live only in fable. Fairies, as in the days of yore, are our intimate friends. Their gifts are treasured by the descendants of the receivers of these fairy favours, and there are amongst us some who still believe in the existence of the little people. We have heard a man, holding a responsible public position, telling a well-known American publisher of a sweet melody his aunt had heard played around her at a burn side in his native county, in the North of Scotland. The harmony of sound dwelt in her mind, so she returned home lilting the cadence of this weirdly-beautiful music, and jotted it down and rendered it to her family circle.

"Do you mean to tell me you believe in fairies?" asked the American, gazing in astonishment at the learned Scotsman. The Highlander replied as gravely as if his confession of faith had been challenged, "Of course I do." So it is not only in the *Ultima Thules* of our coasts, removed from the advance of civilisation, fairies still are credited with existing, but men in all the stir of this twentieth-century life, with its accumulated wealth of scientific knowledge, still maintain that we are within sight and sound of the denizens of Elfinland.

Northern fable explains to us how the gay wee folk and gnomes were turned into a useful path, when the world was young. Odin had spied from his high seat wicked dwarfs and sprites in mischief. He sent Hermod, the Flying Wind, to bid them speak with him. The "light elves were surprised at the summons, not quite knowing whether to feel honoured or afraid. However, they put on their prettiest manners and went clustering after Hermod like a swarm of lady birds." They were very inquisitive, but became awed when they saw Odin in the Judgment Hall, and hung back in the doorway, peeping over their comrades' shoulders. They had to be beckoned to, two or three times, and finally shoving one another, and whispering timidly, they reached his footstool. "Then Odin spoke to them in calm, low, serious tones about the wickedness of their mischievous propensities. Some of the very worst of them only laughed in a forward, hardened manner, but a great many looked up surprised and a little pleased at the novelty of serious words, whilst the light elves all wept, for they were tender-hearted little things." Odin named the two dwarfs whom he had seen murdering the wise man, and so pleased were they at their fame they leapt up and danced and boasted of their misdeeds. Then Odin thundered with disapproval at them, condemned the wicked dwarfs to live far underground from henceforth, and throw fuel upon the earth's fire; those who had only been impishly mischievous were to hammer in the gold and diamond mines, and only at night return to breathe the upper air. Chattering with fear and rage they departed, but the light elves stood with their joyous faces bedimmed with tears and begged Odin to forgive them, as they had done no one any harm. Sage

Odin asked if they had ever done anybody any good, and they confessed, with innocent candour, that they had never done anything at all. " You may go then," said Odin, " to live amongst the flowers and play with the wild bees and summer insects, but you must find something to do or you will work mischief like the dwarfs from idleness."

The elves explained they were such foolish little people and had no one to guide them, so Frey, the genius of clouds and sunshine, was sent for, and promised to teach the brainless, useless elves to burst the folded buds, to set the blossoms, to pour sweetness into the swelling fruit, to lead the bees through the honey passages of the flowers, to make the single ear a stalk of wheat, to hatch the birds' eggs and teach the young to sing. Delighted were the elves at the course of study that Frey suggested, and away they went with him to Altheim, and so the frivolous elves became our tricksy, pretty fairies, who, like Puck, sing merrily:—

> " In the cowslip's bell I lie,
> Where the bee lurks there lurk I."

Oberon and Titania and all their mimic train dance lightsomely before us in poetry and romance, for they have been made into familiar spirits for us by pen and brush. These are the inconsequent fairies of northern fable, but those denizens of Elfinland who live in Scotland have been described by the people preserved in folk lore, and also ministers of the gospel have written what they believe to be facts about these fairies. The Rev. Mr. Kirk of Aberfoyle, at the beginning of last century, published a book describing these contrairy sylvan pigmies. He says: "They are a kind of astral spirits between angels and humanity, being like men and women in appearance and similar in many of their habits. They live in subterranean habitations, and in an invisible condition attend very constantly on men. They are very fond of human children and pretty women, both of which they will steal if not protected by some superior influence. When people offend them they shoot flint-tipped arrows, and by this means kill either the persons who have offended them or their cattle. They cause these arrows to strike the most vital part, but the stroke does not visibly break the skin, only a blae mark is the result visible on the body after death. These flint arrow heads are occasionally found, and the possession of one of these will protect the possessor against the power of these astral beings and at the same time enable him or her to cure diseases in cattle and women."

Another divine in 1670, Lucas Jacobsen Debes, in his description written from Thorshaven in the Faroes, complains " of the fairies disturbing his congregation and sometimes carrying off his hearers." The Rev. Lucas must have surely delivered very spiritual discourses when he drew around him those teasing elves, who could lend their aid when they listed as a choir invisible. Perhaps his congregation were not averse to these fairy visits, or did not object to being lifted from out of hearing of the good man's lengthy discourse. We must bear in mind that the people of previous times led less artificial lives than we do. As a modern writer says: " When we were children we did not say at such a distance from the post-office or so far from the butcher's or the grocer's, but measured things from the covered well in the wood, or by the burrow of the fox in the hill. We belonged then to God and His works and to things come down from the ancient days. We would not have been greatly surprised had we met the shining feet of an angel among the white mushrooms upon the mountains—for we knew in those days immense despair, unfathomed love, every eternal mood—but now the draw-net is about our feet."

As we have grown in civilisation we have lost many instincts once granted to mortals. We have undoubtedly acquired knowledge, and thereby power, on many subjects, but our progenitors, along with untamed races and animals, had faculties of sight, smell, and hearing which education and indoor life has blotted out from our list of attainments. They lived close to nature, who was a kind old nurse to the children who cuddled close to her, and she gifted them with a keener range of vision than we possess. They therefore may, for aught we know, have seen face to face their good neighbours of whom so much has been said and sung.

To account for the deep-rooted belief still extant that fairies appeared on this earth, the theory grew that the tradition of existence arose from their likeness to the dwarfish Lapps who were forced by conquering tribes to seek shelter in the remote fringes of our country. This ancient race of swart Lapps, to judge by the remnant left, had many tastes and habits in common with the fairies. "They are always represented as living in green mounds. They pop up their heads when disturbed by people treading on their houses. They steal children. They seem to live on familiar terms with the people about them when they treat them well. A Lapp is such a man," says J. F. Campbell in his *Popular Tales of the West Highlands.* The Lapps who survive in the Far North set great store on their deer for food and drink and clothes, and for motive power. The merry brown fairies had an aversion to the killers of deer, and they milked the hinds and lived on familiar terms with their cherished four-feeted people as do the Lapps.

Another Mr. Campbell (J. S.) in his *Superstitions of the Highlands and Islands of Scotland,* mentions that in an account of Gaelic superstition and belief the first and most popular place is to be assigned to the fairy or elfin people, or as they are called in both Irish and Scottish Gaelic, the *sith* people, that is the people of peace—the still folk, or the silently-moving people. The antiquity of the belief is shown by its being found among all branches of the Celtic and Teutonic families, and in countries which have not within historical times had any communication with one another. Of all beings with which fear or fancy peopled the supernatural, the fairies were the most intimately associated with men's daily life. In the present day, when popular poetical ideas are extinguished in the universal call for "fads," and by cold material laws, it is hard to understand how firm a hold a belief like this had upon men in a more primitive state of society, and how unwillingly it is surrendered. Sound is a natural adjunct of the motions of men, and its entire absence is unearthly, and unnatural, and not human. The name sith without doubt refers to the "peace" or silence of fairy motion, as contrasted with the stir and noise accompanying the movements and actions of men. The German "still folk" is a name of corresponding import. The fairies come and go with noiseless steps, and their thefts or abductions are done silently. "Sometimes, indeed, the elves make a rustling noise like that of a gust of wind, or a silk gown, or a sword drawn sharply through the air, and their coming and going has been indicated by frightful and unearthly shrieks, a pattering as of a flock of sheep, or the louder trampling of a troop of horses. Generally, however, their presence is indicated at most by the cloud of dust raised by the eddy wind, or by some other curious natural phenomenon, by the illumination of their dwellings, the sound of their musical instruments, songs, or speech." Our conventional modern idea of fairies is something very brisk and active, but the little folk who moved without disturbance, though they darted hither and thither full of pranksome mischief, journeyed so silently, the only trace of their progress heard by the plodding wayfarer being the jingling of their bejewelled bridles. These restless but *still* people evidently *glided*, for there is a verse of a Gaelic song describing the triumphant progress of a ship:—

> " Onward past Greenock,
> Like the deer of the cold high hills,
> Breasting the rugged ground
> With the hunter in pursuit.
> She sailed with *fairy* motion."

This shows how with what graceful quietness the sylvan pigmies skimmed along. Their title of " good neighbours " reminds us of Border parlance when the key of the East of Scotland was Berwick. It was well to be on good terms with the powers that be. The red-roofed borough by Tweedmouth changed hands frequently, so with diplomatic blarney it was styled "our good town of Berwick." "Never speak ill of the deil" is a proverbial maxim, for mortal man never knew when his Satanic majesty might be within earshot. The invisible and alert fairies for the same reason were always mentioned with a honeyed tongue. The wily, knowing not where they might be lurking, were careful to call them "the good neighbours," "the honest folk," "the little folk," "the gentry," "the hill folk," and "the forgetful people," the "men of peace." Klippe is the Forfarshire name for a fairy. A well-known minister of the Church of Scotland related, this century, at a dinner in Edinburgh, how his father had met a klippe in a bare moorland in Forfarshire, a little brown-faced elf who started up on the path before him, walked before him awhile and then vanished.

It was the poets who gave the "still people" the epithet of "the crew that never rest." Our good neighbours from pigmyland seem to have been divided into various classes or degrees. There were trows or drows, which derivation Scott explains "being a corruption of duergar or dwarf, and who may, in most respects, be identified with the Caledonian fairies." It was the skow or Biergen trold that Lucas Jacobsen

Debes complained of disturbing his congregation. They belonged to the woods and wilds and appeared in caverns and subterranean haunts like the German kobold. Belonging specially to Scotland was the bogle, a mixture of the friendly fairy with a dwarfish grotesqueness of figure and nature. Then also there was the Pan-like ourisk of the Highlands, a hairy lubber, who hanging about homesteads watching the humans at work, wished to emulate them and became harnessed for mortals' use. He was trained and bribed by food, becoming readily a hewer of wood and carrier of water. His undulled savage instincts allowed him to foresee coming events, so he was credited with repaying his patrons by giving timely warning. He worked hard for small reward, for the wages he craved for most was the milk of human kindness. He was easily offended and strong in his likes and dislikes. It became in ancient days a fashion for the great houses to encourage an ourisk to attach himself to them, and in course of time he became part of their entourage and grew into the banshee, the spirit who wailed to them of coming evil. All is fair in love and war, and knowing that the hairy ourisk was both liked and feared, Scott mentions that the celebrated freebooter, Rob Roy, once gained a victory by disguising a part of his men with goat skins so as to resemble the ourisk, or Highland satyr.

The kelpie, the water-witch, who lurked by Border water-sides, and took the toll, ever and anon, of a human life, was a Caledonian spirit. The kobolds, common in German lore, like the duergar Sir Walter tells us of, haunted the dark and solitary places and were seen often in the mines, where they seemed to imitate the labours of the miners and sometimes took pleasure in frustrating their objects and rendering their toil unfruitful. Sometimes they were malignant, especially if neglected and insulted; but sometimes also they were indulgent to individuals whom they took under their protection. These trows and bogles, kobolds and kelpies alluded to, were more of the goblin kind than the merry-making, aerial people we connect with the name and nature of fairy. These lightsome, tricksy folk were again sub-divided. There was the English pixie, the Scottish brownie and spunkie, full of merriment and teasing propensities. Mr. Campbell, in his *Superstitions of the Scottish Highlands*, explains " a difference of size as well as of name has led to these being described as separate beings, but they all have so much in common with the Celtic fairies that we must conclude they were originally the same." "The true belief is that the fairies are a small race, the men about four feet or so in height, the women in many cases not taller than a little girl. At one time the elves are small enough to creep through keyholes, and a single potato is as much as one of them can carry; at another they resemble mankind, with whom they form alliances and to whom they hire themselves as servants." These honest folk, by whatever name they were known, could be helpful to the mortals around them if so minded. They liked to earn their title of good neighbours, though whimsical and capricious in their friendship. When they arrived at a new place of residence they were wont to bless their new home, repeating the following couplet full of sweet content, a hopeful motto for mortals who change their dwelling:—

> "Though good the haven we have left,
> Better be the haven we have found."

Even in the glaring, uncompromising light of to-day, in the westmost British Isle there are those who believe in the existence of "the crew that never rest," for in *The Celtic Twilight* Mr. Yeats tells how he himself has seen the inhabitants of the " dim country." He went with one who had the second sight to " a notable haunt of the forgetful people, a shallow cave amidst black rocks, with its reflection under it in the wet sea sand." There he was granted a sight of the tall queen in gleaming garments. In the Celtic gloamin', now as in the light of other days, the fairies have changed little in their dress—green as a rule being their favourite colour. There is also a grey called the fairies' grey, a glaucous green like the leaves of the eucaliptus. It is the women who adhere mostly to the verdant hues, for the men in some places are called the little red men, their clothes being dyed with crotal from the lichen, and their cowl-like hats were scarlet. They love showy splendour, and the gorgeousness of their apparel in their pageants impressed beholders.

The following information concerning the government, etc., of fairyland is taken from Aytoun. " The queen of fairyland was a kind of feudatory sovereign under Satan, to whom she was obliged to pay *kane* or tithe in kind, and as her own fairy subjects strongly objected to transfer their allegiance, the quota was usually made up in children who had been stolen before the rite of baptism was administered to them. This belief was at one time universal throughout all Scotland and still prevalent at the beginning of this century. There was also a king of elf-land. From the accounts extracted from or volunteered by witches, etc., preserved to us in justiciary and presbyterial records he appears to have been a peaceable, luxurious, indolent personage who intrusted the whole business, including the recruiting department, to his wife. We get a glimpse of both their majesties in the confessions of Isabella Gowdie in Aulderne, a parish in Nairnshire, who was indicted for witchcraft in 1662. She said, " I was in Downie Hills and got meat there from the queen of the fairies, more than I could eat. The queen is bravely clothed in white linen and in white and brown cloth, and the king is a braw man well favoured and broad faced. There were plenty of elf bulls rioting and skoyling up and down, which affrighted me."

The Rev. Mr. Kirk, who seems to have had intimate knowledge of the wee folk, states " that in fairyland they also have books of various kinds—history, travel, novels, and plays—but no sermons, no Bible, nor any book of a religious kind."

Despite their endeavours to be useful the fairies, from all accounts, only succeeded for all their fussing in hampering work. They seem by some tales to stand for a personification of busy-bodies. Little good ever came of having the fairies for helpers. "No wise man will either desire their company or their kindness. When they come to a house to assist at any work the sooner they are got rid of the better. If hired as servants their wages at first appear trifling, but will ultimately ruin their employer. The benefit of their gifts goes ultimately to the fairies them-selves or (as it is put in the Gaelic expression) 'the fruit of it goes into their own bodies.'" This statement seems ungrateful and thankless, for there are stories of fairies repaying debts in truly generous fashion: not only is the loan of meal returned, but the fairy bowl of ground grain returned never grows less, till some discontented member of the family grumblingly asks if they are never to have aught but barley meal to the end of their days, and when next the goodwife dips her hand into the barrel, behold, it is empty, for the invisible host around had hearkened to the malcontent and withdrew their favour. The fairies, with these alert ears and easily-offended natures of theirs, proved stern monitors. If mortals were not grateful and content they listened to their fretful repinings and gave them some cause to complain. When people grudgingly said that their healthy children might be even rosier, or disparaged their crops and herds and complained they might be still better, the fairies heard, and the apple-cheeked children paled and grew weakly, the heavy grain was shaken, a murrain fell on the beasts in their fields. It was reported that the fairies who blighted the enviable things mortals had despised reaped the benefits that the human beings were deprived of. Their kine grew fat, while those of the grumblers were wasted and lean. Their harvests were safely garnered and the farmers' full ears of corn were winnowed by the winds. The fairies, naturally, when such rich prize-money fell to their share, eavesdropped muchly. Fairies seemed, out of a spirit of mischief, not that they needed food, to have a fancy to raid dwellings and take what they liked. Handmills they were partial to, and when their women ground the corn, they sang at the task so blithely, mortals who walked over the green mound where they dwelt paused and listened and learned their songs. Friday was a day on which the fairies seemed to hold revel above ground, raid houses in open daylight, and investigate the very dishes preparing for dinner. No wise person named Friday but called it " the day of yonder town," for the fairies preferred it so, and it was well to curry favour with these tricky good neighbours. When they journeyed in companies they took advantage of the wings of the wind to speed them and so wheel them past the plodding traveller, who heard the laughter of the still folk go and the jangle of the bridles of their caprisoned steeds as they glided by. They are perverse pigmies — they arrive from the *west.* Usually invaders borne on the tide of conquest have come from the other side of the compass, but, on the contrary, soulless men of peace journey withershins about, and come from the sunset land. There is a verse of an old song bidding mortals—

" Shut the North window
And quickly close the window to the South,
And shut the window facing West—
Evil never came from the *East.*"

The god of light and warmth rose in the east

—the Star of the East guided the Magi, and as Christianity grew the direction from whence the dawn arose was looked on as sacred and safe. Although fairies in the tales we love with their opportune gifts invariably prove valuable friends, their help and comradeship were not sought after. Mortals dreaded to meet them on the " day of yonder town " flitting along on the eddy of wind. Firm was the belief that they would capture a mortal and take him prisoner to their bloodless, soulless kingdom. Music and meat and dancing they had, but these did not tempt prince or peasant. A Mayo woman in this young century of ours has told the gifted young writer of to-day, Mr. Yeats, how she has seen the denizens of Elfinland. " Her thoughts and her sights of the people of faery are pleasant and beautiful too, and I never heard her call them the fallen angels. They are people like ourselves, only better-looking, and many and many a time she has gone to the window to watch them drive their wagons through the sky, wagon behind wagon in long line, or to the door to hear them singing and dancing. They sing chiefly, it seems, a song called 'The Distant Waterfall.' They are always good to the poor, she said. If you do good to them they will do good to you, but they don't like you to be on their path." This path was the track they pursued when taking an earthly journey. More than one traveller has returned from their realm, and the story of Thomas the Rhymer's visit to Elfland is specially worth recording, for as Scott says, he dwelt on Thomas of Erceldoune's history as the "oldest tradition of the kind which has reached us in detail, and as pretending to show the fate of the first Scotch poet whose existence and its date are established both by history and records. But the legend is still more curious from its being the first and most distinguished instance of a man alleged to have obtained supernatural knowledge by means of the fairies." Thomas the Rhymer, one of the earliest of Scotland's versifiers, lived at Erceldoune, by the Leader. Owing to his love of lonely wanderings and communing with nature, he acquired the reputation of being a master of magic. "Divested of fable," says Sir Thomas Dick Lauder, "we should probably find him standing forth as a very prominent figure amidst the worth and talent of our countrymen." There, by the bogle-haunted Huntly burn, under the shade of the Eildon tree (now gone, but a cairn marks the spot where it grew and flourished), the Laird of Learmont lay ruminating one day when there appeared before him a wondrously beautiful lady. An ancient ballad tells us—

> " Her skirt was o' the grass green silk,
> Her mantle o' the velvet fine;
> At ilka tett of her horse's mane
> Hung fifty silver bells and nine."

She informed him she was the queen of fair Elfland, and looking on her, True Thomas doffed his cap " and louted down to his knee," and she carried the learned poet away there and then from the magically-cloven Eildon's slope, showing him many strange sights as they journeyed and many devious routes, till the queen drew his attention—

> " . . . to that bonny road
> That winds about the fernie brae?
> That is the road to fair Elfland
> Where thou and I this night maun gae."

> " It was mirk mirk night, and there was nae stern light,
> And they waded through red blood to the knee;
> For a' the blude that's shed on earth
> Rins through the springs o' that countrie."

They came at last to the fairy kingdom where revelry and dancing were the order of the day. Thomas passed so delectable a time that when the queen asked him how long he thought he had been there, he calculated some seven days had been passed chasing the golden hours with flying feet. He could scarce believe the beautiful sovereign when she assured him he had been gone from earth five years and two. Every seventh year the fairies had to pay to Satan a life, and the clever little people preferred that this debt should be paid by a mortal. Thomas of Erceldoune being a well-favoured-looking man, the queen advised him to flee, sure that the devil's ambassadors would claim so comely a captive. As a parting token of goodwill the elfish queen bestowed upon him a gift which he fain would have declined—namely, with a tongue which could not lie. The Rhymer protested that such a present would be highly inconvenient, explaining blunt veracity at market, kirk, court, or ladies' bower, would make him unfit to bargain successfully, or appear well before his neighbours in church and finish his career as a courtier. But the queen pressed this honest-tongued favour upon him, and so for ever after he spoke with unflinching candour, earning for himself the title of True Thomas. He was also invested with a supernatural discernment which penetrated the veil of the far-off future. Thomas returned safe from the incessant beguiling revelry of Fairyland, and with his tongue of truth he uttered prophecies still quoted. Many other people have declared that they too had dwelt with the fairies, but none were men of outstanding ability and importance like the Laird of Learmont.

The speed with which time in fairyland flies was not only Thomas the Rhymer's experience. A miller, so folks tell to-day, fell asleep on a grassy mound in a peaceful strath in the north. The little folk took him off, and on the anniversary of his capture, when the elves danced again of a June night among the nodding grass and the bluebells, his friends reclaimed him. He awoke as from a pleasant dream, shouldered his sack, and went off towards home. None of his neighbours could persuade him he had been asleep for twelve months. He thought they were jesting till, nearing his cottage, his wife met him with a child clinging to her skirts. He had left a year-old baby when he went to fetch the sack of meal home. He returned to find the baby a prattling, toddling wee thing, and not till then did he realise that the fairies had held him a twelvemonth in thrall.

Gifts received, or spoil acquired by mortals from the little people, are treasured amongst us. The elves were hospitable. They liked their human neighbours to eat, drink, and be merry with them. Endless tales are told of them biding their big neighbours, who strayed in among them while they were carousing, to partake of their feast. A goblet in which they were drinking a "richt gude willie waught" in their sovereign's honour roused the envy of a Musgrave. He rushed in, seized the glass, mounted in hot haste and galloped away with his stolen trophy. Some authorities hold that the good folk are not averse to crossing running water. It is only a wicked class of them whose powers are blunted by traversing flowing streams. But legend tells us Musgrave pressed his steed towards the brook, for he knew if once he forded it, the rain of fairy flints showered at him, and all pursuit, would cease. His terrified courser, spurred by steel and fear, leapt the water. Safe across the river he paused, and borne on the breeze, Musgrave heard his despoiled pursuers forgivingly sing—

"Joy to thy banner, bold Sir Knight,
But if yon goblet break or fall,
Farewell thy vantage in the fight,
Farewell the luck of Eden Hall."

In the Musgraves' Cumberland home the illicitly-obtained "luck" — a glass goblet — remains intact, carefully preserved.

The Macleod clan appear to have been specially favoured by the fairies. One of their name entered an elfin brugh when a banquet was in progress. He was warmly welcomed. "Here's to you, Hugh," "I drink to thee, Hugh," they cried, bowing to him and quaffing from a glittering cup. When the bowl was passed to him, instead of proposing a toast, Hugh bolted with it, eluding the elusive little folk, who loosed their dogs to overtake the thief, but he escaped. He had a narrow escape. He heard the hound called Farvann shouted for. If this four-footed guardian of the fairies had captured the false Macleod it would have gone ill with him, for the spunkies' dogs, from all accounts, resembled Sherlock Holmes's baffling quadruped enemy, the Hound of the Baskervilles. The elfish tyke, like themselves, was *green* of coat and as large as a two-year-old stirk. Its tail was sometimes curled over its back like a pig's, sometimes plaited into a long wisp. The fairy hound was either kept tied as a watch in the brugh, or escorted the women on their search for cows to milk. Sometimes it was allowed to roam alone, making its lair in clefts. Like the fairies, it moved silently, but for all its gliding gait, the print of its paws, as big as a human hand, were found on mud or sand or snow. Its voice was sonorous and far-reaching, being heard even by those sailing on the seas. It paused between each bark and at a time gave vent to only three roars. Its baying struck terror into the pursued, who was invariably overtaken and destroyed after the third bark if he had not hidden himself from his unearthly pursuer. Hugh Macleod, we learn, escaped from Farvann, and the goblet he had stolen long glittered at Raasay. To Macleod of Dunvegan was given by an elfin mistress the green fairy banner still preserved in the hoary castle in Skye. It is a useful possession, swaying even the tide of battle, gaining the victory, not for the strong, but for the weaker, oppressed side, by the supernatural power in its folds. Three times in dire emergencies it may be waved with success. Twice it has been flung to the breeze, and its third miracle has yet to be wrought. Meanwhile, to-day, it lies secure in the Macleod's thousand-year-old stronghold, awaiting to flutter once more in some great strait, when its owner is fighting back to the wall. Perhaps its third charmed wave may be kept till the long-prophesied battle on the Clyde is fought, the battle which Thomas the Rhymer awaits, when he will rouse from his slumber, and ballad story tells how—

> "When Thomas comes with his heroes
> The day of spoils will be on the Clyde.
> Nine thousand good men will be slain
> And a new King will be set upon the throne."

In bygone times, when fairies were seen by the people, or wheeled in invisible, aerial armies around, doughty warriors faced these uncanny, supernatural little folk with unflinching bravery, deeming them foemen worthy of their steel. The number of the host of fairy enemies made up for their small size, and a regiment of pigmies armed with deadly weapons might well make the stoutest knight quail.

The fairies, like the gipsies, though they were said to have many bairns of their own, had a longing to steal human babies. To guard the infant and even its mother from being borne off from the humblest of cottages to the fairies' palace, cautious and incessant watchfulness was needed. Cold iron fairies misliked, and the newborn babe and its mother were protected from the elves by iron. The fairies were so far honest that when they abducted an infant they left in the cradle one of their own. This changeling never throve; it became an ill-conditioned, weird child. When it grew up its ease and grace in dancing, and sometimes its musical excellence betrayed its origin. Music was a gift the fairies possess—one they sometimes gave to mortals. The strains of pipes and songs were ofttimes heard by men, though they saw no player, and this bears out the idea of the Rev. Mr. Kirk that the elves were astral beings who floated around invisible, or appeared as they willed to the dull-eyed inhabitants of this world. Those who have ears to let them hear can execute tunes, curious and uncommon, which they say they learned from the spirits. For instance, there is the "Song of the Hillock" which was heard by a woman who, noticing her dog with ears cocked, transfixed on a knowe, followed him and hearkened. The fairies were butter-making, and as they churned, lilted. The woman remembered the rune, and "for three generations, *i.e.*, till our Victorian era, it was chanted." Macrimmon, a piper to Macleod, acquired his skill from the good neighbours. He was going across the mountains to a pipers' competition and stumbled into a fairy dwelling. The dance-loving "men of peace" were kindly disposed towards the eager boy-musician and gave him a magic black chanter, which remained an heirloom in his family, and their skill was such they outrivalled all pipers, so that "their fame will last while wind is blown into sheepskin."

The fairies were fickle in their bestowal and withdrawal of favours, and changeable as an April day.

"Rain and sun,
Little people at their meat;"

says one adage, but from all the lore regarding them (and there is no small measure thereof) they seemingly have given many benefits to man—some trophies, as the cup at Raasay and the luck of Eden Hall had been filched from them—but the priceless fairy banner remains at Dunvegan as a visible proof of their goodwill, besides the Macrimmon's musical talent, and sweet melodies they taught us. Except the indictment that they stole children and lifted also older mortals, the fairies were truly good neighbours—freakish, and sometimes interfering, but as a choir invisible beguiling the road, hospitable, repaying what they had borrowed with lasting lavishness, although their offerings might be in a curious guise, or handicapped by some seemingly whimsical restriction. Then we all are indebted to the fairies for the tales they bequeathed to us, for their legends are a rich possession. It has added a joy to childhood, and fairy lore has entwined itself from nursery days about our hearts in ever-green sprays. Its teaching has borne good fruit in after life, impressing goodness and mercy upon us more than many sermons. In fairy literature we learn that the presumptuous are brought low, while those whose gentleness and kindness of heart have made them side with the weak and oppressed are exalted and rewarded. Little deeds of kindness, little words of love, like bread cast upon the waters, return to the heroes and heroines of fairy story, not even after many days, but is immediately garnered. The fairy tales teach us to be considerate and well disposed to bird and beast. The saying, a little bird whispered to me, is a relic of those times when the beasts of the field and the fowls of the air spoke in a language intelligible even to human beings. The feathered, winged creatures were the swift and sure messengers in an age before post and telegrams.

Fairy godmothers have become proverbial for their ways of pleasantness. They could, with a wave of their wand, bridge over difficulties and assist their favourites. They lent prompt aid to the helpless and needy, encouraged the sat-upon but deserving ugly ducklings of the flock, and gave them fine feathers. Fairy lore teaches the child to be friendly and generous to the feeble and despised. The decrepit crone, helped over a slough, casts off the weather-worn cloak and stands in sparkling raiment beautiful to behold, ready to fulfil the wishes and load with favours the mortal who did not despise her in her wrap and wrinkles. The proud girl spurns and ill-uses the four-footed creatures, while another, rich in heart if not in goods, bestows sympathy and assistance on some timorous beastie. Soon the purse-proud, arrogant lass is brought low and the kindly one exalted. The heroine of the fairy tale shares her crust with the hungry, makes them welcome to her few possessions, and in the end finds her gifts are returned with a thousandfold interest. This sharing their all was the symbol of a truly generous disposition.

The wealthy might scatter largesse and think they had done nobly, though their well-filled pockets were not perceptibly lighter, but the "mite" given by those who owned but a mite was taken in good stead. Sir Launthal set forth in search of the Holy Grail, and rode far afield in his pursuit all gaily bedight in his golden armour. He gave from his well-filled coffers with a liberal hand, but no heavenly blessing fell upon him. Only when returning, stripped of his wealth, humble of heart at his failure, the knight, wearied and saddened by his fruitless search, near to his own gate gave to a diseased beggar half of his remaining bite and sup:—

> "He parted in twain his single crust,
> He broke the ice on the streamlet's brink,
> And he gave to the leper to eat and drink."

The cup of cold water he received back was the long-sought-for Holy Grail. While he stared amazed, he heard from the whilom beggar's sacred lips that it is not what we give, but what we share with another's need that is doing His will:—

> "Who gives himself with his alms feeds three—
> Himself, his hungering neighbour, and *Me*."

In the fairy stories which Grimm and Hans

Andersen have written for us, we learn this simple creed—that the gift without the giver is bare. The fairies see the sham through all the cheap outward show, and they teach in their tales what cost Sir Launthal a toilsome journey to realise. Impishly mischievous, fickle as April weather, were fairies, if the tales be true told by those who aver they had met with them; but in Grimm or Hans Andersen their capriciousness disappears, their helpful services shine forth in no uncertain, will o' the wisp gleams, but with a steady brilliance which lights the way through seductive snares. The fairy lore shows the benefit of sweet content as well as strict observance of the given word and punctual fulfilment of promises. Cinderella, dazzled by the brilliance of the ball, forgot to leave at midnight as her godmother had commanded, and lo! her regal trappings began to fade, but she made haste to redeem her promise, and was requited. People had to consider well who was to be bidden to the feast in the days fairies flew around. They must leave out no one, however shabby or old, or despise the seemingly worthless gifts. The neglected one might have some friend in the court at Elfinland, and the seemingly small offering brought to christening or marriage might be a magnet to wealth and honour to the receiver, a talisman worth more than the bejewelled donation the wealthy brought.

To fairies in times past mortals were indebted for valuable service rendered—and whether it was dull-headed human beings, or the sprites themselves who bequeathed to us fairy tales, their lore has been and still is a goodly heritage we all enjoy and can profit by the lesson their tales teach. "Those that see the people of faery most often, and so have the most of their wisdom, are often very poor," says a writer of our century. And, after all, can we come to so great evil if we keep a little fire on our hearths and in our souls, and welcome with open hand whatever comes to warm itself by our hearth, and whether it be man or phantom, do not say too fiercely, even to the dhouls themselves, "Be ye gone."

CHAPTER V

FISHERMEN'S SUPERSTITIONS

" Green earth has her sons and her daughters,
And these have their guerdons, but we
Are the wind's and the sun's and the water's,
Elect of the sea."

SWINBURNE.

THE sons of the sea rovers, though aware of the danger of their calling, were never afraid to face the billows. They saw their fathers set forth, ofttimes never to return, but, undeterred by knowing full well that after a life of toil a watery grave awaited them, they too invariably adopted the same precarious profession. In the West of Scotland a pretty legend exists to account for this hereditary perverseness. A man had become enamoured of a mermaid whom he first espied combing her " ling lang yellow locks " while he was wandering along the shore. He was warned by a sea god that swift death awaited him if he pursued his suit. Finally he was persuaded by threats and bribes to turn his attention back to a lass of his own race who had tarried for him inland. The lover told his adviser, though he would do as he was bidden he would not forget the halcyon days of summer he had spent, lingering by the tide with the fair lady of the sea who had entranced him. The merman, struck by the landsman's fondness for all that appertained to his watery realm, promised him that his descendants would likewise be ocean lovers. Before the earth dweller turned his steps inland to woods and fields the sea god baptised him with the splash of a wave. His race in this country grew and increased, and sure enough, the fascination for the salt water never left them. They stand on our shores to-day, like the deep ocean, dressed in dark blue, scanning with keen eyes the dancing waves, and never, how far inland they may go, able to cast off their desire to roam over the world of waters. The sea is to them as a woman whose beauty attracts, but her favours or her frowns alike bring trouble. Her smiles lure the sailor forth, and then she swoops down on him like a fury. In the West of Scotland, to ward off disaster from the siren of the seas, children, before they were twenty-one days old, had their right hand baptised in the waves. If done at the flow it averted death by drowning. The watery grave of those who by misadventure had their tiny baby fists dipped into the briny, hungry waves at ebb-tide is chronicled to-day.

The fisherfolk remain strangely conservative in their ways, though their minds are enlarged, their wits sharpened by their voyagings. A modern writer explains that one reason why the Russian peasants have remained so stolid, dumbly enduring abuse, is because in their country they had no seaboard, therefore never any new ideas come to them. They have no wish to penetrate beyond their forests, and this stay-at-homeness has kept them for generations unprogressive. The population on our shores, on the other hand, was for ever open to new impressions, and with wits alert ready to receive such. Our fisherfolk are more than usually intelligent, keeping abreast of the times, although they rigidly adhere to certain customs and seemingly childish superstitions. They judge of the atmospheric changes by symbols taught to their forebears in ages past. The fleecy, mackerel-backed cloud which indicates more than a capful of wind, and seagulls flying inland when skies are fair, they note as a storm warning. Sir Patrick Spens, King Alexander's skeely skipper, misliked seeing " the new moon wi' the auld moon in her arm," and sure enough, he and all the good Scotch lords who sailed with him from Norroway, " never mair cam hame." A halo round the sun or moon was not welcome; brocks they are called.

> " When the sun sets in a brock
> He'll rise in a slauch;
> But if the brock dees awa'
> Ere he sets in the sea,
> He'll rise in the morning
> Wi' a clear e'e,"

says one adage. Rainbows were not welcome unless they came when there was clear shining after rain. The broken ends of the bow foretold uncertain weather, as also did the " merry dancers " — the *aurora borealis*. The fishers noted the coming storm in the cat's tail. When grimalkin was playful he chased his own brush. The furniture cracking, the beasts scratching themselves, told of a change. The tribe of the sea read the face of the waters as if it were a printed book. They were forced to be weather-wise long before the days of barometers, barographs or telegraphed storm warnings. They had to study the ocean and sky not only for food and money, as the farmer does, but for their safety when on the deep. Harvesting the halesome faring of the sea costs lives of men, however skilful mariners may be. Harbours before last century were few, and the crafts of days of yore seemed, to modern ideas, but poorly equipped to face the billows. The ancient Britons had learned to stretch the skins of beasts on a slim framework, and these cunningly-fashioned wood and hide boats imitated the shape of the sea birds which, while resting on the waves, breasted their undulations. Even now on the west coast of Ireland, where the long rolling billows of the Atlantic break, the boats used there are these light coracles. They face the swell and the surf and float over the mountainous sea with a bird-like grace and ease, whereas a modern-shaped, low-bowed boat would fill and swamp. The Vikings built their galleys high-prowed, shaped like swan or gull. Far indeed over the ocean they sped if the surmise in regard to that round tower at Newport on America's shore be as Longfellow sang of it and antiquarians conjectured, namely, that it was built by some venturesome Berserker whom the "wind of God" had sent scudding across the Atlantic before Columbus's day. There the skeleton in armour built the lofty tower for his wife's bower on the fringe of the undiscovered great world. Despite their long voyages the Vikings and our mariners of old were discreet. They rested in winter. All their weather-wise lore could not preserve them from the season of gales, so in this land statutes were in force which forbade the lieges of the kings of Scotland risking their lives sailing on the seas in the darksome, turbulent months between St. Jude's Day and Candlemas.

Some of the fishermen's customs still in vogue date back to prehistoric times. A rite of those who live by the sea was practised on our western shores till lately. The people by the ocean depended on the great waters not only for fish but for manure for their fields of grain, so on Hallowmas, and some say on St. Columba's Eve, they offered libations of ale and gruel to the god of the sea. A man at midnight between Wednesday night and the eve of Maunday Thursday walked waist deep into the tide and chanted the following prayer, while those on land took up the refrain:—

> "O God of the sea,
> Put weed in the drawing wave,
> To enrich the ground,
> To shower on us food."

So we see along our coast there lingers the ritual of fire and oblations, and the fisher who pleads from the sea sustenance looks from his boat at the monoliths which, looming through the mist, look "like a company of stolid carlines met in council." The sea god to whom toll was paid was in some parts called Shoney. It was a chill period in which to walk into his territory and pay tribute. The people were wretchedly poor on the land side of his sovereignty, but they combined to brew ale for the ceremony. They held a prayerful service in a church by the shore first, then proceeded to watch the beaker of their home-brewed ale being poured on the waves while they chanted the lines with their chosen agent, after which they returned to the church, where a candle burned, and at a signal its feeble light was extinguished. Then, armed with provisions not wasted on Shoney, they adjourned to some field, where they ate and drank and sang till dawn. The church, like most since

Columba's time, when he, the pioneer missionary, first lit the eternal light of Christianity on his lone islet on the western fringe of Scotland, had evidently decided to pander to the god of the sea and allow his worship.

A custom dating back to dim, distant days is the annual burning and making of the clavie at Burghead, in Morayshire. And what was the origin of the word clavie, or the meaning of the belief adhering to it, no one knows. On Yule night, according to past dating, they make this unique clavie, *i.e.*, a barrel sawn in two, to the lower half of which there is affixed a long handle. In the manufacture of the clavie it is all-important that no iron hammer is to be used, but a stone does in its stead. The barrel is filled with wood dipped in tar and piled so as to form a pyramid with a hollow in it. Into the centre of the pyre is placed a burning peat. Another rule as well as that no metal hammer is allowed, is that no light be set to the tarry pile except by a brand already ablaze, and a modern match is sternly excluded. The clavie set aglow, a further libation of tar is poured upon it, and, regardless of flame and smoke, a man shoulders the flaring clavie. If he falls, or even stumbles, it augurs ill for the town, so a bearer strong thewed is carefully selected. When a bearer is wearied, or is choked by smoke, another is always there eager to carry the clavie. One after another they step forth until the town has been encompassed by the flaring barrel. Then they march to a hillock called the Doorie, where on a stone the remaining blaze is placed and more fuel added. In past centuries it was fed all night long till a new day dawned, but in this hurrying age time is money to the fisherfolk, so now they let the fire burn on the altar but for a brief space and proceed to roll what remains of the smouldering barrel adown the western slope. On its last journey a scramble is made by the onlookers, for every one in the crowd wishes to seize a brand from the descending, dying clavie. One secured, the possessor bears it home in triumph, for it is credited with the power of preserving those under the roof tree that shelters it from ill for a year. In bygone times one strong man was selected to carry the clavie around the town, but now the post of honour is shared among several of the able-bodied. Also in days of yore the ships in the harbour were visited by the clavie. Indeed as late as 1875 the clavie was carried on board one vessel about to make her first voyage. Grain was showered on her deck, and then with a sprinkling of fire and water she was named *Doorie.* The town has grown greatly and assumed bigger proportions than the fiery clavie can encircle, so only the older part is girded by the burning barrel. What the meaning of this clavie ceremony is we can only conjecture, from some of its rites, that its origin was in the pagan past, and instituted by an extinct race to protect their homes and persons by sea and land.

Peculiar to another seaport town is a rite unique as that of the clavie. At Queensferry, within ten miles of Scotland's capital, every year saw the upkeeping of a singular practice. It is thought to commemorate the arrival of Margaret Atheling and her marriage with Malcolm Canmore. It was lucky for that widowed king that so well-dowered, well-born a princess was driven by stress of storm to seek shelter in the Firth of Forth at his very doors, for in those days the "king sat in Dunfermline tower, drinking the blude-red wine." He could not leave his distraught realm to seek a helpmate. England barred him to the landward, and it needed time and fine weather to journey overseas to woo a fitting wife. Margaret Atheling, by one chronicler, is reported to have been vivacious, but we know her best as the queen muchly given to good works—a most zealous Catholic, intolerant of other sects. She thought the lives of her monkish emissaries were endangered traversing the Firth, so at the strait where her vessel had first anchored, she instituted a boat to cross in, and the place was named after the royal lady. At the village of the Queen's ferry, the port of the passage between Edinburgh and Dunfermline, yearly, in early August, on the day preceding the fair, the inhabitants bedecked the burry man. The chiefmost figure was a lad dressed in loose garments, which were covered over with burrs from the thistle or burdock (the *arctomus bardana*). They grow near Hopetoun and further up the Firth at Blackness in plenty, and were collected for the occasion—"so essential are they deemed to the maintenance of this curious ceremony, the origin and object of which are lost in antiquity and long ago foiled the antiquarian research of even Sir Walter Scott. The custom in question can be traced back to the period of the last battle of Falkirk, for an old woman of eighty, whose dead mother was aged thirteen at the date of the battle (1746) stated that the observance has been unaltered from then till now (1885)." When the burry man, encased as if he were in armour in his suit of close-sticking burrs, grasping staves adorned with flowers, marched through the town, shouts were raised at every door, and the dwellers came forth with greeting and money to wish him well. The revenue thus accrued was divided between the chief actor and the lads who helped to yearly resurrect the burry man of Old Queensferry.

Conservative in its ways, sticking to dress and vogues of its own, is the fishing village of Newhaven, almost within hail of "High Dunedin's" castled rock. Villas have encroached on it and nearly crowded it into the Firth, by whose margin it grew many centuries ago. Some think the originators of these sterling fisherfolk were of Flemish extraction. Howbeit the wives, creel on back and much be-petticoated (wearing sometimes fifteen short skirts) cry their wares, caller o'o and caller herring, with clear-voiced strength through Edinburgh's grey streets, and their men in the blue clothes bring a smack of the salt water into twentieth-century Princes Street. Newhaven was a fishing hamlet in James III.'s reign, and his son, liking the looks of the tribe of the sea who dwelt near to his " House of Kings " at Holyrood, established a rope walk there and finally enlarged the place, for this gallant Stuart king was the first after Bruce to foresee Scotland, hemmed in by our auld enemies, the English, would have to form a navy if she wished to become a power and hold her own among the nations. He added houses to the fishing village for his workmen. Instead of being known as Our Lady's Port of Grace, by which title it had heretofore been named, James's dockyard was dubbed The New Haven. Blackness, so much further up the long-armed Firth, was the old port which, till then, had done much trade; for it was nearer Dunfermline and Linlithgow, where the Court held its revels. Holyrood became, as Stuart rapidly succeeded Stuart, a favoured residence, and when James resolved to found a navy, he determined to see his ships grow rib by rib under his own eye. To escape from toils of state, from the revels he perforce held, he with his train of nobles ambled down by Bonnington to his chosen haven, and watched the men at work and heard their hammers ring and their saws rasp. James's interest in the building of his huge ship, the *Great Michael*, gave an impetus to the sea village he had patronised. It was endowed with certain burghal rights, and in its midst was built a chapel called St. Mary's. We cannot picture the jacketless, blue-dressed fishermen, or their buxom, independent wives worshipping as Romanists. However, a generation later, along with the timber for Mary of Lorraine's palace on the castle hill, came Lutheran literature, which landed close by Newhaven. The fisherfolk, early in Reformation times, became staunch Presbyterians. Yet so tenacious are the lilts of folk lore, in their children's songs there remains still a trace of the Catholic ways and days. The wee lasses and lads at one game sing—

> " My coffin shall be black,
> Six angels at my back,
> Two to sing and two to pray
> And two to carry my soul away."

These fisher-bairns, playing with the cordage on the shore, looking out on the devouring sea which has been often in generations past their paternal breadwinners' grave, end this rhyme peculiar to Newhaven with the verse—

" Ding dong knell,
The passing bell,
And good-bye to you, my darling.
Bury me in yon old churchyard
Beside my own dear mother."

The father's resting-place was doubtful, but in the God's acre in the midst of the village the sturdy wives, the true helpmates of the fishermen, were of a surety laid. In this enclosure, at the times of burial there, Mrs. Cupples, writing in 1888 and recalling Newhaven as she had seen it in her childhood, says: " In the grass-grown, ancient enclosure just now referred to, when a funeral took place, it was very noticeable how the coffin was borne along, in crowded procession, on poles held by the chief mourners; and how, as it passed within the said old burying-ground, each follower dropped into a plate beside the entrance his contribution in silver, its purpose being to defray all necessary expenses." " Dwelling," says a writer in 1865, " only a few bow-shots from the metropolis of an ancient kingdom, this people remain isolated, apart, distinct in costume and dialect, in manners and mode of thinking. The customs, laws, and traditions of their forefathers appear as if they had been stereotyped for their use. To think of dogs is unlucky; of hares terrible! Should a reference be made to a 'minister' as such, vague and undefined terror fills every bronzed visage, as he should be spoken of only as 'the man in the black coat'; and Friday is an unlucky day for everything but getting married, and to talk of a certain man named Brounger is sure to produce consternation." This John Brounger, who is unmentionable, was an age-enfeebled fisher of Newhaven, who, when too frail to go to sea used to beg of some of the able-bodied boys in blue oysters from their catch. If they refused his demand he cursed them and wished them on their next trip ill-luck. The curse was sometimes fulfilled, so to propitiate him he as a rule got his toll of oysters as an established right. Hence it came to pass if a fisherman said, John Brounger is in your head sheets, or aboard, the crew pulled in their nets and putting out their oars circled round thrice to break the spell.

The strapping women of Newhaven and Cockenzie have so big a share in the work of earning a livelihood, when they hear of one of their men marrying out of their circle they exclaim contemptuously, "Her! what wad she do wi' a man that canna win a man's bread?"

In a community that seldom marries with the outer world, the same names are common, and the fishermen are distinguished by having their wives' Christian names added to their surnames, such as Maggie's Flucker. An old ballad tells of a Newhaven wedding, on the lucky day:—

> " Weel Friday cam', the growing moon
>   Shone beautifully clear,
> An' a' the boats wi' flags were drest
>   Frae Annfield to the pier.
> An' Doctor Johnston, worthy man,
>   Had twa-three hours to spare,
> Sae he toddled to Newhaven
>   An' spliced the happy pair."

Above Newhaven's red roofs there appeared, till recently, a giant willow. The legend of its origin has been preserved. It grew to be a towering tree seen from afar on the summit of the Whale Brae, a steep street where once an inquisitive monster of the deep ran ashore. Judging by the girth of the willow it must have been long, long ago that a fisher-wife with her bairn, cradled in the skull of her creel, sat one spring waiting for her man's sail to heave in sight. She would doubtless be busy knitting, and, like her Newhaven sisters, would be an accomplished weaver of wool, so she could scan the Firth for her gudeman's craft, or turn and look on her babe while her quick fingers all the while webbed the wool into warm garments for her sea-rover. At last she spied his boat come raking through the spray, and rose to shoulder her creel and meet it, when a blizzard loured down and hid the Firth from sight. When the squall had swept past no sail was visible. She realised what had happened: she was a widow and her bonnie bairn orphaned. She sank in a swoon of despair by its osier, fishy cradle. The wild winds of March were heavily laden with icy cold from the north. On the track of the blast that had wrecked the boat and blighted the life of the fisherman's hostages to fortune, as the new-made widow lay unconscious, clasping her babe, there came a snowstorm and swathed the grief-smitten woman and her little child in a white pall. The bank below whose bield she had sat slipped and buried them. The fishers, when the snows melted, sought and found her and her babe on this hill by the sea above their Port of Grace, now a gardened suburb. They buried them in the old churchyard—the churchyard which is now a drying-green wedged among houses bordering on the electric-carred roadway. It was spring-time, warm days had come, and the wicker creel the baby had lain in had been freshly woven. It had been cast aside, but one of the wands rooted in the vernal brown earth had sprouted. An old woman from the village noted it and prophesied that the wand from the new-made wicker cradle would grow into a great tree—a landmark for the homeward-bound mariner. Generation after generation of fisher-lads would sport below the tree or climb its branches. This strangely-planted willow would grow and flourish while the trade and prosperity of the village increased. But the soothsayer added it would fall either when the fishing trade left Newhaven, or when boats, great decked boats fit to face the German Ocean even in winter, set sail from the harbour over which the tree kept sentinel. When the willow grew hoary with years, houses compassed it about, but with the title deeds of the site on the brae head called " Willow Bank " went instructions that the tree was not to be destroyed. The better to preserve it, it was girded round with an iron railing, and its legend put into rhyme. In the mid-Victorian era trawling began to lessen the fishermen's gains. Down one wintry night came a great arm of the watchful willow, and the men taking this as an evil omen, were with difficulty restrained from attacking the trawlers to save their sea trade. Luckily for law and order, for generations they had at Newhaven been shepherded by good divines. Mr. David Johnston of St. Ninian's, North Leith, for fifty-nine years (1765-1824) had ministered to them. When Leith was in a panic over the threatened invasion by the renegade, Paul Jones, he not only exhorted his people to pray for protection, but, being a practical man, who believed that the Lord would the better help those who tried to help themselves, he urged the fishers to form themselves into a band of sea volunteers, and he was the first to enlist. He may have married the young fisher-wife who watched from the green hill by the sea and saw her husband's boat sink; at any rate Mr. Johnston knew the willow which grew into a landmark for the home-steering rovers. When the tree broke in twain the Rev. James Fairbairn administered to the spiritual welfare of the red-tiled village which Edinburgh, "flinging her white arms to the sea," had encroached on. He reminded the people there was a saving clause in the soothsayer's prophecy.

When she saw the wand, tenacious of life, first shoot, she said it would survive till the trade left the village, *or* till decked boats bore with their crews out of harbour. He urged his people to set to work to get bigger craft. He opened up the means for them to do so. He loaned money when they collected enough to meet him half-way. He borrowed more on his own security for them. Gradually a well-equipped fleet of big brown-sailed, decked smacks, headed by the *James Fairbairn*, sailed from Newhaven, and so prosperous were they they elbowed the small boats out of the harbour. When the last of the obsolete smacks was finally superseded, the huge, prophetic willow, first watered by the young widow's storm of tears, fell in the sixties of last century, its mission fulfilled.

Sailor-men all along our coast share a dislike to meeting when the Blue Peter is flying, or mentioning while under canvas pigs or parsons. At Cockenzie a stranger's well-intentioned "Good-morning" to a fisher on his way to his boat would make him remain at home, as it was interpreted to be an evil omen. Superstition makes the fishers clap a guard on their tongue, for God's name taken in vain, specially on entering or leaving a port, will make the crew shudder and cry for cold iron to grasp to remove the ill-luck. How they ever get to sea at all with pigs and cats to cross their path is a wonder. A hare too is an unchancy beast to meet when seaward bound. In this our present century, one day in the *Scotsman* there was the notice of a case of malicious mischief. Some youths had caught a wounded hare and stowed it away in a fisherman's boat, so that when he set sail it would inevitably be found. The witch-absorbing quality of a hare, the universally-credited unluckiness befalling any one if it crossed their path when setting forth on a venture, is well known. This hare the lads secreted on board the smack, when its limping forth from its hiding-place would strike terror into the crew, for who would, however prosperous the weather looked, sail in a witch-ridden boat? So serious were the consequences of this prank, the originators were had up before the sheriff for "conspiracy." Friday is avoided by the fishermen for setting out on any enterprise except on a matrimonial venture. Maybe the idea of being dangerous to sail upon had arisen as it was the day the fairies were rife, but now, in times of keen competition, men have to hoist their sail on a Friday. The lottery of fish-catching, its precariousness, the hazards on the changeful sea, fostered a belief in the sailors of omens, for which they still look before they depart from the firm land. "When a fisherman left his house to proceed to his boat it was considered unlucky to call after him, even though he had forgotten something essential. If he was a Shetlander he was 'particular as to meeting a person by the way lest they should have an evil eye, or some accidental malformation.' It was considered a good omen to meet an imbecile or a person deformed from the birth." These were called by the Shetlander Gude's poor, and being of God's making they were not despised. After meeting one such when setting sail, if the ship prospered, to God's poor was given an *aamas* or *kjoab*, *i.e.*, a dole. As in the case of John Brounger of Newhaven, folk lore or superstition made the fishers give of their store to the poor, the needy, and those whom Providence had afflicted. "It was believed any one who crossed a fisherman's path when he was on his way to his boat intended to scathe him. When the fisher came to the spot where his way had been crossed, he took out his knife and scratched the ground in the form of a cross, uttering the word 'twee-to-see-die' and spat on the place. The sign of the cross was considered an antidote against the intended evil, and the spittle an emphatic expression of contempt for the unchancy hag."

The short sward of the links shorn close on the east coast of Scotland by the keen winds is useful for other purposes than golf, ancient though the royal game be. May is a month evidently from pagan times that is sacred to many rites. To the Douny Dell in the Bay of Nigg in Kincardineshire there was a narrow way from the mainland called the Brig of ae Hair, which led to the green knowe which was all but an island. Across this hair-breadth bridge in the merrie month the young folks went to carve their names in the turf. There was a well there dedicated to St. Fittick, and it was evidently deemed expedient to let him know whose names were associated, not writ on water, but cut side by side on the grass on his semi-isle.

Herrings in folk lore seem to be quick to hear, and discordant notes jarred on them. The church bell of St. Monance (which hung on a tree) must have sounded harshly, evidently not attuned to musical ears, for when the herring were around the coast it was not rung because it was averred the silvery harvest of the sea were frightened from the shores of Fife by its jangling knell. Herring, according to the fishers, are among the blessed in this world, at any rate they make for peace, fleeing when they hear a war of words, and withdrawing from the land where quarrels are rife. Where blood is shed they do not return that season. Their mode of procedure should make the fisherfolk beware of entrance to a quarrel. The sea-ploughing Manxman adds in the litany after the prayer for the fruits of the earth a petition for the continuance of the blessings of the sea, for the harvesting of herring is as important to them as the garnering of grain. They are a truly religious community, our fisherfolk. The dangers of their calling make them realise how unstable is their tenure on this life, and during it how hard it is to procure a livelihood. They taste to the bitter dregs the sorrows of the sea; but they scan it with calm, unflinching gaze. Nature has whispered the secret to the trees how to withstand the gales. She has made them throw out their roots in the direction from which the prevailing winds assail them, grip the ground and defy the assaults of the blasts. So with the fisherfolk. They know their storm of fate will inevitably come from the turbulent temper of the sea they love, but from generation to generation they have so builded up their forceful characters that even women and children look with unflinching bravery over the ocean, prepared to bow but not to break before the felling blows of fate; and the men, however loud the winds howl as they speed over the rising waves, lustily sing:—

> " We put our trust in Providence
> And trust His gracious aid."

In many parts of our shores before the men set out on their quest they gather in the church for a farewell service, and in some parts the minister blesses the nets and prays that they may be filled.

The sailors the world over believe in the sweet little cherub which sits up aloft to watch over Jack at sea. He has not to climb very high on the fishing boats, but he has these mariners' fortunes at heart. Watts, the great artist of our day, realised this, for one of his most popular pictures is that of the curly-headed cherub fluttering over the green waves. In his plump little hands he holds the end of the brown lines. His knees are bent as if asking a favour. "Good luck to the fishing," he pleads.

> "Weel may the boatie row
> That wins the bairnies' bread,"

sing the fisherfolk, watching the brown sails scudding along. Every hope for man's good is a gain, and the fairies and folk lore teach us a benison falls also on well-wishers, and so the song ends by asserting—

> "And happy be the lot of all
> That wish the boatie speed."

CHAPTER VI

FLOWERS AND BIRDS

" The rough bur thistle spreading wide
  Among the bearded bear,
I turned the weeder chips aside,
  And spared the symbol dear."

BURNS.

To turn from sea to land, round the flowers and trees about us a wealth of legend clings. They are not only rooted in our affections as friends of our youth, but our country's history is wreathed in them. The Rose and the Thistle now twine together, and they foster under their prickles the Shamrock. The Rose's entrance into Scotland was not under popular auspices. It was that Hammer of the Scots, Edward I., who had a golden rose for his device, perhaps derived from his mother, Eleanor of Provence. The Thistle resented intrusion, but had for a time to succumb to the Rose. Gradually the queen of flowers became the emblem of England. It grew into the gage of Red and White when Henry VI.

chose the one, Edward the other, and round these rival roses raged civil war. The scented petals of both were dyed in the life blood of Englishmen. Badges were a necessity, for before the days when uniforms distinguished warring companies, when mail veiled friend from foe, some mark had to be worn on the helmet. In old-fashioned gardens a rose flourishes of blended colours called York and Lancaster, a symbol of the unity of the two rival factions when Henry VII. married Elizabeth of York, engrafting one of the chief surviving branches of the White rose tree upon the rooted stem of the Red flower, and out of that peace-making union sprang the heraldic rose of the Tudors. The shamrock, so folk lore says, became the symbol of the most distressful country in St. Patrick's days. He was preaching to the Irish and could not explain to his converts the doctrine of the Trinity, so he illustrated his meaning by plucking the lowly trefoil at his feet, and "he assured his hearers that as in the distinctly three cleft leaflets there was truly but one leaf, so might this great doctrine of the Three in One be in poor fashion believed and accepted in humble faith." As to the thistle, "poverty, ill-luck, enterprise, and constant resolution are the fibres of the legend of this country's history," says Conan Doyle, while another modern writer endorses the statement, "cold and poverty and storm are the nurses of the qualities which make for empire." The Scots' land, that "barren ridge of hills between two inclement sea-ways," as Robert Louis Stevenson calls his native country, elected for its emblematic flower no summer-blooming, sun-nursed rose, or fond as she is of doctrine did she choose a plant explanatory of religion, but history or tradition fixed for the Spartanly-nursed north on the hardy, prickly thistle whose seeds spread on the wings of the wind and which roots and flourishes in apparently stony soil. Cackling geese saved sleeping Rome, likewise the thistle gave Scotland timely warning, and her people were grateful to it for averting disaster. The invading Danes had stolen on the sleeping camp of opposing natives, but the latter were florally guarded. The thistle undertook to act as a barbed wire entanglement. Nature reared it in the dark ages when modern tactics were undreamt of. The thistle's lancet-shaped foliage made the stealthily-creeping, bare-legged Danes give tongue. The Scots heard their smothered curses, awoke, and armed. That is how, some say, the repulsing thistle was adopted as Scotland's insignia, along with its defiant motto, "Ye daurna meddle wi' me," which became in the sleeker Latin tongue under the British Solomon's orders, "*Nemo me impune lacessit.*" In James III.'s reign the symbol of the thistle was first mentioned among the crown jewels, and on the marriage of his son to Margaret Tudor, Dunbar indited a prophetically-named poem "The Thrissel and the Rose." This bride brought about the union of the sister kingdoms, although at the time of her marriage no seer foretold that she brought along with her dowry the succession to the crown of England. Her great grandson followed the Stone of Destiny to Westminster when her niece Elizabeth died. So, henceforth, the armed Thistle and the gentle Rose grew side by side. The wild thistle had been associated before this with fair garden flowers, for it had stood shoulder to shoulder with the lilies of France.

> "If you would France win,
> Then with Scotland first begin,"

was an olden saying, and ambassadors knew how true an adage this was, for when the Rose was a dreaded flower, encroaching on the Thistle's domain, France was her ally and helped to keep the Rose's roots from spreading beyond her legitimate kingdom. The Stuarts, a century after the Rose and Thistle had entwined together, for their special badge adopted an oak leaf in grateful recollection of the sheltered hiding-place Charles II. had found on the tree. The leaf proved to be a somewhat prophetically transient emblem, lacking the tenacious staying power of the thistle. The Jacobites sadly watched it, like their hopes, fade and wither. From the broom which Geoffrey of Anjou plucked and put for cognisance in his helmet his race took their name of Plantagenet. The Forbes in the north have it also for their badge, for the heather and the broom are closely associated together with the hills of Scotland. White heather from its scarcity is prized. Some folk say it is the print left by the resting fairies. When the heather was on fire the blaze meant in days of yore, unsheathed swords in the Highlands. It was a beacon for the clans—

> "To arm and make ready then,
> Sons of the mountain glen."

In Scottish song we meet ofttimes with the

birks. On the grave of true lovers whom death has not divided the birk and the briar flourish together, as when the actors in the tragedy of *Douglas* are laid to rest.

> "Lord William was buried in St. Marie's kirk,
> Lady Margaret in St. Marie's quire,
> And out of her grave there grew a birk
> And out of the knight's a brier."

When the Black Douglas came along full of vengeance, for had not his daughter's lover fought and slain his seven sons—

> "He pull'd up the bonny brier
> And flang it in St. Marie's Loch."

To "pu' the birks sae green" is an ill omen. So we read in one version of "The Dowie Dens of Yarrow"; in others it is heather. There was a wife who dwelt by Usher's Wells in ballad story—

> "A wealthy wife was she,
> She had three stout and stalwart sons
> And sent them o'er the sea."

They returned to her from the dead and in their hats were branches from a birch.

> "It neither grew in syke nor ditch
> Nor yet in any sheugh;
> But at the gates o' Paradise,
> That birk grew green eneuch."

Though presaging ill in dreams to see it green it

is a popular favourite, so it may well grow gracefully on its silvery stem, humbly drooping its branches at Heaven's gate.

The cross of the Saviour, tradition says, was made of the bourtree (elder). It is not misliked, often being planted about dwellings, but it is deemed unlucky to cut it. Before trimming it to shoot out anew in spring, it was customary to mention the fact to the free-growing elder in the following words:—

> " Bourtree, bourtree crooked,
> Never straight and never strong,
> Ever bush and never tree
> Since our Lord was nailed on thee."

That rhyme exonerated the gardener from ill intent. The ever-quivering aspen twists, so the story sayeth, for ever restless with the shame that it was the tree Judas chose. The poet sings in " Gloomy winter's now awa " of " the silver saughs with downy buds," the precursors of spring gleaming and shining against the grey skies of February. Saughs have stood for sorrow ever since by the waters of Babylon the harps were hung on their branches. All the flowers which Goethe classes as " the beautiful hieroglyphics of Nature, by which she indicates how much she loves us," are easily understood by unlettered children, and round the blooms they love the best they have woven garlands of association which remain perennial throughout life.

Daisies, the wee modest crimson-tipped flowers, smiling up into little faces, have been always prime favourites. They are forged into chains by tiny fingers. Bairnwort it is called in the borderland, for it is indeed the children's playmate. "The gowans fine" are dear to Scots the world over. Whether the gowan is the larger, long-stemmed species, or the bright-faced, simple floweret—the day's eye—smiling up from out of the carpet of grass at us from dawn to dusk, from earliest spring to the season's end, we know not. It is a lesson to many—humble, contented, with its unflinching gaiety, its bright eye, always admired and popular with young and old. The anemone of our April woods was patronised by our good neighbours the fairies. Inside its drooping bells, which promptly closed around them, they took their beauty sleep, clasped in its petals, when weary of dancing in the glades or wind-swept moors. Some old people remember in their time Easter eggs were invariably dyed by its juice, and at the spring festival of the church this blue "Pasque" flower, as it was called, was worn. "The pretty name 'windflower,'" says Mrs. Miller Maxwell in *Children's Wild Flowers*, "is as old as the centuries, for it comes to us echoing down from that mysterious Egypt where, while regarded with tenderness, it yet appeared as the emblem of sickness and suffering. Later on the Romans, ever borrowers of other customs, wore wreaths of anemone only, which they called Egyptian garlands, when entreating the favour of the gods for some beloved sick one's loss. Constantly we find joy and sorrow intermingled, for this same anemone, if mixed with other blooms, was worn at feasts and merry makings, these wreaths having been hung round the statues of Venus, their particular patroness. A special significance was given to the first anemone of the year. The flower was plucked with reverence and religious ceremony, and the magic words repeated, 'Anemone, I gather thee for remedy against all disease,' and then the blossom was put carefully away and kept in its hiding-place till illness threatened."

A companion to the fairy-cradling anemone,

which also, slender of stem, braves the breeze on the wind-shorn uplands and decks the sea-braes revelling in the briny air, is the bluebell. It nods among the grasses on the auld fail dyke, roots on the sandy bank by the wayside, and is a welcome flower where'er it blows. It is lengthily named by botanists *campanula rotundifolia*, but its folk-lore name of harebell tells how it tinkles warningly to the beasts who crouch in their lair near to where it springs, and it sings to them a soft, low melody. Scott speaks of—

> " The slight Harebell that raised its head
> Elastic from her airy tread,
> For waving on its thin tall stem,
> It bends before the gale which breaks
> The wind-resisting forest trees."

The bluebell's elegant, thimble-like flowers the fairies loved, and pranked along on pageants becapped with harebell hats. The white species is considered lucky when found growing wild. The commoner blue was said to be worn in honour of St. George, but St. George's Day is in April, and the old rhyme likely enough applies to the wild turquoise-coloured hyacinths which at this season Tennyson says are like the heavens upbreaking through the earth.

Ash trees were lucky to have planted around

a dwelling. They defended the householder from witches, but as a green shade they are unsatisfactory, being not only loth to clothe themselves with leaves, but shedding them early in the season again. Throughout the Highlands, often the very stones of a deserted cottage or a clachan of hill-side homes have been carted away to mend walls, and a grassy mound and a few lonely ash trees only remain to tell where there had been many a poor black cottage grimy with peat smoke. The old folks, the kind folks who loved the place of old are overseas. The rowan, the ash's relative, is nurtured too by the cottage door. Its red berries make necklets for the children. There lingers since the Roman era a belief in red as an amulet, a preventive of evil. Coral was worn for this reason and holly berries prized therefor. Tennant in his *Tour through Scotland* mentions that farmers placed boughs of the mountain ash in their cow-houses on the second of May to protect the beasts from malign influence. It was an antidote to all the wiles of witchcraft. A branch of it above the dairy doorway kept the milk sweet. The staff of the churn was made of it so that evil spirits would play no pranks with the butter. The ash was sought for for a Yule log, for the giant tree Yggdrasil which roofed the gods in Asgard was the ash.

Christianity adopted the flowers and used them as emblems of their saints, flowering at the time of their particular festival, so many flowers became herbs of grace bracketed with holy names. For instance, June 24 is St. John's Day, and the yellow flower (*hypericum perforatum*) became associated with that feast time. The common fern on St. John's Eve was pulled in the height of summer when witches were abroad; it was a panacea against their incantations. St. Peter's wort was the cowslip, and the bunch of yellow blooms his keys. Southernwood, whose sweet scent savours of a country church, has also the name apple-ringie. It is the herb of St. Ninian, Saint Rin's wood. The "apple" is from an old word, aplen, for church, or house of the church, so maybe St. Ninian grew the fragrant wood at his home, and it smells still of the kirk and summer. Many flowers with lady in their name had been adopted by the Church and consecrated to the Virgin. The crown imperial lily has its blooms turned down and in the depth of its bell-shaped flowers are great spots. It is said to have assumed this shape for shame at not having bowed to the Lord, and the drops in the depth of its cup are the everlasting tears it sheds in contrition. The flowers throughout the year make us enjoy the friendship of the seasons. They are, as "one who dwelleth by the castled Rhine" said, "stars that in earth's firmament do shine." They lighten and gladden our way, and no place is so exposed, so stony, but they thrive and glow, in some cases turning wastes into fields of cloth of gold. No wonder Linnæus fell on his knees and gave thanks for the "mountain gorses ever golden" so gallantly blooming the whole year long.

There are delicate flowers which cannot face the nipping winds, but peep out at us from nooks where they are cosseted by stronger brothers, or seek shelter in the woodland dells where "spunkies dance." The fragrant violets' scent recalls—

> "The sweet South,
> That breathes upon a bank of violets,
> Stealing and giving odour."

Its companion, the primrose, has become the badge of the Conservatives on the supposition that it was Beaconsfield's favourite flower. For on April 19 it is torn from its home on dells and braes and sent up to towns in ton loads to do honour to the great leader's name, yet only once in his writings did D'Israeli mention the pale floweret and pronounce it good for flavouring a salad. Forget-me-nots of Heaven's divinest blue mark the streamlet's course, where they grow profusely "for happy lovers." Blue is the sweetest colour that is worn, green is the emblem of grief, and yellow is forsworn or false, so lovers' knots and lovers' bouquets are of the forget-me-not's true blue. Every flower we tread on, from the butter-coloured celandine, the herald of wild spring, which appears before even the "maids of February" whiten the garden with their snowy bells, all through the seasons till "the reed is withered from the lake and no bird sings," there is on moor and bosky shelter some plant abloom, some tree overhead, which folk lore and association has endeared to us. As well as legend and wood myth to interest us, beauty to please the eyes, the flowers have been given powers to heal bodily ailments. Nature has placed the antidote near the bane. If you have not grasped the nettle like a man of mettle, but handled it gently and been stung for your pains, the soothing dock is near. There is a balm as well as beauty in every flower. Foxgloves relieve the heart-sore. The poppies wave among the wheat—together grow the tall, cultivated staff of life, and, planted by Nature among the straight cereal, ripples the scarlet wave of sleep. As Hamilton Aide says:—

> "When on some fevered bed perchance,
> The corn will not avail,
> Nor wine nor any potions deep,
> To call one little hour of sleep
> Over the eyelids pale;
> 'Tis then those useless scarlet coats
> (Like some of human kind),
> Prove their strong hearts can soothe distress,
> For all they wear a gaudy dress
> That flutters in the wind;
> Their sundried leaves have not in vain
> Outlived the harvest day,
> If life has gained one hour of peace,
> If troubles for a moment cease
> Under the poppies' sway."

The queen of flowers, the rose, stands for the emblem of silence—*sub rosa* is a secret message. Eros in Greek mythology presented a rose to the god of silence, and from the East comes another proverb, " A little bird told me." It is a saying often in our mouths to-day, and in ballad story we read how Johnnie of Breadeslee, when he and his "gude graiehounds" lay aweary with the chase and glutted with venison they were shot by the seven foresters, Johnnie cried:—

> " O, is there nae a bonny bird,
> Can sing as I can say,
> Could flee away to my mother's bower
> And tell to fetch Jonnie away?
> The starling flew to his mother's window stane,
> And it whistled and it sang,
> And aye the ower word o' the tune
> Was 'Johnnie tarries lang.' "

The bird as a messenger is a relic of the days when man and beast spoke together. Birds were the swift messengers that sped from country to country. They flutter about us still, for any one who reads the fables of old finds from east to west our little brothers of the air bulk largely in fairy story. In Egypt to-day they say God blesses the house on which the birds build, and we look for a stroke of good fortune when the swallow nests in the eaves. In Scotland the old "doocot," surviving the manor house to which it belonged, stands alone in a field. Superstition would not allow of its being destroyed despite its feathered inmates being voracious poachers among the farmers' new-planted crops. It is still held it forbodes ill to strip the pigeon house, so the feathered poachers have a roof kept over their heads though the chimney stone is cold in the manor. Piebald birds or beasts, by reason of their "kenspeckle" coats, are subject to notice, and round them the country people built a host of superstitions. The pert pyots (*anglice*, magpies) foretell, according to their number, birth, death, marriage, or an heir:—

> "One's joy, two grief,
> Three's a wedding, four's a birth."

Or,

> "One bodes grief, two's joy,
> Three's a marriage, four's a boy."

Sir Humphrey Davy believed in two magpies promising well for anglers in spring. It is held to be unlucky to see one, the reason being, so Sir Humphrey says, in cold and stormy weather one only leaves the nest in search of food:—

> "Man on the piet horse,
> What's good for the kink host?"

Dr. Jameson says a friend of his often was asked, and the rider of the parti-coloured steed used to amiably order, candy. Folks in spring when they first hear or see summer's heralds note how to meet them:—

> "Sit to see the swallows fly,
> Stand to hear the cuckoo cry.
> Is the foal before its mother's eye,
> A happy year will come and fly."

In Scotland the cuckoo is called the gowk, and in some rhymes it is well not to stand but to "gang and hear the gowk yell." To hunt the gowk on April 1, is synonymous with making a fool of yourself, for seldom is it heard till May. A cock crowing with its head into the door of a house was said to be a sure token that strangers would soon cross the threshold. So prevalent was this belief, when thus warned, the goodwife would proceed to tidy up the house and prepare, like Leebie in Thrums, to receive visitors. A hen that crowed brought ill luck to the owner, and when it evinced such an unwomanly voice it was promptly killed. "Whistling maids and crowing hens are no canny about a house," says the Scotch proverb. A bird coming into a house was as a rule thought to be propitious; but if a cuckoo cried from the chimney, it was held to be a certain sign that death would be below that roof-tree soon. One thing in regard to this latter superstition, the sign would seldom be heard, for the bird who has no sorrow in its song, no winter in its year, despite its impudence in ridding itself of the troubles of rearing its children, is a shy bird seldom seen, unique though its marvellous monotone is, listened for as the advent of summer. Whatever quarter you face when first in the sweet of the year you hear the cuckoo, in that direction your steps will be led during the coming twelve months. The robin, from its sociability and tameness, as well as from the prominent part it played in happing up the babes in the wood with leaves, is a prime favourite. Its breast, legend says, was dyed red in its attempt to pluck the crown of thorns from off the Saviour's brows. The robin by its mythical good deeds has immunity from molestation from mankind. Even nest-hunting boys revere the home of the red-breast. In some cases folk lore has acted as a prevention to cruelty to birds, for rhymes threatening maledictions on those who harm popular birds stay the hand of evil-doers.

> "The laverock and the lintie,
> The robin and the wren;
> If ye harry their nests,
> Ye'll never thrive again,"

is one verse which Scotch boys believe in. Another verse says:—

> "The robin and the wren
> Are God Almighty's cock and hen.
> The martin and the swallow
> Are God Almighty's bow and arrow."

Jenny Wren was always coupled with Cock Robin in the popular mind, and the bustling, diminutive bird was under the Church's protection:—

> "Malisons, malisons mair than ten
> That harry the Ladye of Heaven's hen."

Although folk lore preserved some birds, it by some curious quirk has harboured the superstition that the yellow hammer (the yorling or the yite in the Scots tongue) drank a drop of the devil's blood on May morning. It is persistently persecuted because of this belief. With its unlucky yellow plumage, its jerky, uncertain flight, it is held to be of peculiar extraction:—

> "Half a puddock, half a toad,
> Half a yellow yorling,
> Drinks a drap o' the deil's blood
> Every May morning."

Its note has been translated into a threat of retribution from its patron, the arch fiend:—

> "Cis a cis a see,
> If ye harry my nest
> The deil will harry thee."

Alack! this menace uttered so beseechingly by the blithe little yite (a confiding little bird, for it likes to flutter along the hedgerows as the wayfarer plods his weary way by the dusty highway) does not stay the boys' hand from cruelty. As if to make up from being withheld from plundering the robin redbreast, the yite is sought and, when found, its nestlings are meritoriously destroyed. "When I was young," says Mr. Napier, speaking of folk lore in the nineteenth century, "I was present at an act of this sort, and as an illustration of courage and affection in the parent bird, I may relate the circumstance. The nest, with four fledglings, was about a quarter of a mile outside the village. It was carried through the village to a quarry as far as the opposite side. The parent bird followed the boys, uttering a plaintive cry all the way. On reaching the quarry, the nest was laid on the ground, and a certain distance measured off, where the boys were to stand and throw stones at it. While this was being done, the parent bird flew to the nest and made strenuous efforts to draw it away; and when the stones were thrown, it flew to a little distance, continuing to cry, and only flew away when it was made the mark for the stones. This was but one of many such torturing scenes yorlings were doomed to suffer, but they have survived, and their confidence in man is unshaken, for it is as bold as the robin in seeking human companionship." The plover was long detested in Scotland. Its wailing cry of peesweet as it hovers overhead when its uplands are invaded by dog or man earned it this hatred. It is a sentinel against invaders on moors and mosses. It may well cry "about the graves of martyrs," for its warning note brought many of them to death in covenanting times. The dragoons watched the fluttering "teuchet" (as the plover is also called in Scotland) and knew from its movements where their prey hid. Many a covenanting meeting had to disperse because of the hovering, bewailing plover, fearful for their young, clamouring overhead. There is still in some parts a traditional antipathy to the descendants of these birds who thus unconsciously betrayed their companions who lurked among the heather. Leyden alludes to this long-remembered grudge against the peesweet, and, speaking of the Presbyterian fugitives in the wilds, says:—

> "The lapwing's clamorous whoop attends their flight,
> Pursues their steps where'er the wanderers go,
> Till the shrill scream betrays them to the foe.
> Poor bird! where'er the roaming swain intrudes
> On thy bleak heaths and desert solitudes,

> He curses still thy scream, thy clamorous tongue,
> And crushes with his foot thy moulting young,
> In stern vindictive mood."

To turn from superstitions connected with the winged messengers of days of yore to quadrupeds —seers hold it is ill to dream of cows. To meet in the flesh, sheep on the road are good, especially if they pass you on the left. To descend to smaller beasts—a bee, instead of being busy taxing the flowers for honey and wax, flying straight towards one denotes important news a-coming. All children from generation to generation have cherished the same rhyme to exhort the red and black spotted, tortoise-shaped little insect to hasten off whenever they meet it:—

> "Ladybird, ladybird, fly away home,
> Your house is afire, your children at home;
> All but one, that lies under a stone,
> Fly thee home, ladybird, ere it be gone."

In Germany, too, it is met with this startling news. In some places in Scotland where this soldier-coated beastie was made to spread its wings and fly, after it folks sang:—

> "Lady, Lady Landers,
> Lady, Lady Landers,
> Take up your coats about your head,
> And fly away to Flanders."

We also are all brought up in the belief it is daring of the fates to kill a spider, whether it be the diminutive scarlet one or the longer-legged, web-spinning, fly-catching species. As Lord Rosebery says: "It is never wise to explore what has given you pleasure and to endeavour to trace a delightful fiction to the austere sources of fact," and the tale of Bruce and the spider is so woven into Scottish history, I do not think we would believe King Robert himself if he came back and told us it was all a fiction. The persistence of the spider and the lesson it taught the disheartened king, the sermon it preached for all, how to endure and strive till the goal is gained, is a tale every Scotch child is told, and points a moral, and the spider truly adorns a tale. Cobwebs the stirring housewife cannot endure, but she dreads to slaughter the weaver of them. A cricket singing on the hearth is believed to bring riches to the household so favoured.

There is a deal of the doctrine of forgiveness preached in folk lore and fairy tales, despite the cold blood case of the pitiless treatment of the yellow hammer and a hereditary dislike to the betraying plover. It was believed evil went into the lower animals, and by this means they saved human beings by absorbing it. Pigs, cats, and specially hares are beasts full of ill omen and unlucky if they cross the path of landsman or seaman setting forth on a venture. Pussie appears in many rhymes and warnings. There was always a suspicion hanging about a cat of being an assistant at witchcraft, especially if black—a colour associated with the powers of evil, the devil's livery. The grimalkin of the Herd of Men was a somewhat sacred animal in Catholic times. There is a game called the Priest's Cat played by rustics at Scottish fire-sides in the gloamin'. A piece of stick was made hot in the fire and handed from one to another of the circle, idle by want of light, sitting around the hearth.

> "About wi' that, about wi' that,
> Keep alive the Priest's cat,"

one of the party by the fireside said, and passed the brand from hand to hand. When the flame died the person who held the stick was liable to a fine. In days of old, when the priest's cat in the flesh died, there was great lamentation throughout the country-side, as it was supposed to turn into some supernatural being who would work mischief among the human flock, so to keep the priest's live mouse-destroyer in life was a matter of prime importance. Still in some districts people fear to let a cat die in the house, however much of a domestic pet poor "pussie bauldrons" may have been when well. To avoid the catastrophe a bed in an outhouse was made so that it might not expire under the roof tree. To the cat good treatment was as a rule meted out, for from the East it brought with it a halo of sacredness.

With one or two exceptions, in the folk lore of beast and bird we see the initial teaching of the fairy tales to be kind to the lowliest of creatures, for no one knows how good a turn they may be able to do one. The mouse can nibble the lion's bonds, the bird fly over earthly enemies' heads and bring news of friends, forewarnings of raids. Even the plague-carrying, hated rats leave the unsafe ship, telling its tale of rotten timbers to those who choose to listen.

CHAPTER VII

WITCHES AND WIZARDS

> ". . . Graves at my command,
> Have waked their sleepers: oped and let them forth
> By my so potent art. But this rough magic
> I here abjure."
>
> *The Tempest.*

SUPERSTITION, which has been accurately defined as "beliefs and practices founded upon erroneous ideas of God and Nature," clung round the subtle spells, the magically-acquired powers of the uncommonly wise and world-famed wizards of Scotland. Of witches our land reared a full harvest. Shakespeare etched for us amid the storm the three weird sisters seen in lurid glimpses on the blasted heath with their presages and incantations. The generality of prophetic hags were mostly harmless old women bowed down with toil and trouble, mayhap versed in cures, who were doomed to be hunted to death because superstition had led kings and judges to credit these feeble crones with the craft to harm with a "blink from an ill ee." But Scotland's wizards, who loom forth from far-away centuries, were men of thought, cultured, far in advance of their time, well-dowered with property and intellect. Their words have become household sayings, part and parcel of our constitutional credence.

It was owing to the wizard of the nineteenth century, Walter Scott, that much of the old lore of Scotland was in the first place hearkened to, then collected and preserved. That good knight, Sir Walter, the master of romance, had a predecessor, one of his own clan, Michael Scott. This scholarly necromancer, like his successor, Thomas of Erceldoune, was a man of mark in his own time. Their thirst for knowledge, their consequent learning, made them far surpass in thought and sagacity not only their contemporaries, but their era. The coming wizard, Michael Scott, was born at Balwearie in Fife's kingdom early in 1200. A student from his youth, the Scotch laird went to Oxford and on to Paris, where his skill as a mathematician brought him renown, and there also this Fife "lad o' parts" took his degree as a doctor of divinity. Ever unsatiated in the pursuit of study, he went from Paris to Padua and on to Toledo, for Spain was then a lamp of learning to Europe. There his smattering of Arabic acquired at Oxford came to the fore. Reading Aristotle's works in Arabic he began to translate them into Latin, finishing this task in Germany. During his travels he met with Dante, and the Italian poet describes the Scotsman as "meagre of flank," and after many wanderings the lean, spare-formed Sir Michael, the scholarly ambassador, returned to Scotland and settled down in his old family home. There he lived in fame and honour, pursuing his favourite studies, a man who deeply impressed the imagination of his countrymen. The very meagreness of flank of which Dante speaks would help to foster the idea that the far-travelled sage was a necromancer. He ofttimes stood on the battlements of his tower at Balwearie, silhouetted against the clear sky-line, studying the stars, reading the stories of the heavens. His neighbours, high and low, viewed with awe the stately figure of the venerable astrologer, believing he was communing with the uncanny powers of the unseen world, so they dubbed him wizard. He is best remembered around Kirkcaldy, which is close to Balwearie, by the trick he played the devil, who came to claim the recompense of long service. Mr. Geddie says in his *Fringes of Fife*, "That must have been a dull-witted member of the infernal hierarchy who was sent to cope with the shrewd Fife Faust, for he undertook as a last labour to twine a rope out of the sand of Kirkcaldy Bay. Who has waded like us through the dry, loose mounds behind Linktown breakwater must feel sorry for the lubber fiend. He laid him down wearied with his fruitless toil, and Kirkcaldy, listening pitifully to his moan, 'My taes are cauld,' has kept adding stone to stone to its length—an allegory doubtless of the triumph of human will and persistence over the perverse powers of Nature. Some say the deil's dead and buried in Kirkcaldy; others there are who stoutly deny it to this day."

Michael Scott, in ballad story, is said to have turned a monk and died in fair Melrose, where he lies buried with his "mighty book." This book was sought for in his tomb by his successor in necromancy, Thomas Learmont of Ercel-doune. A Lord Soulis was over-skilful in the black art, and none could conquer or kill him, so Thomas unearthed the book of Sir Michael, followed its instructions, and the wicked Lord Soulis, rolled in lead, was burned to death in a cauldron, and the ninestane-rigg, where no heather grows, marks the spot to-day. Learmont of Erceldoune, commonly known as the Rhymer, was, like Michael Scott, a man of wealth and learning. He was a poet, and wandered meditatively by Leader Haughs that looked down into the valley of unrivalled Tweed. He lived, as far as documentary evidence can prove, after the middle of the thirteenth century. The remains of his home at Erceldoune is but a remnant of masonry and stands near to the village of Earlston, which won renown later for the lasting qualities of the ginghams its weavers wrought. Thomas Learmont, having written a poetical romance, *Tristram and Iseult*, became known as the Rhymer. As he solitarily paced, busy "rhyming" and thinking, there grew a belief in his powers of seeing with penetrating vision what was to come to pass. There was a tree on the Eildons below which he sat, and from it it was believed he was borne off to the fairies, where he was inconveniently endowed with the tongue of truth. In Elfinland he learned much of what is hidden from the ken of ordinary mortals. He might, if he came alive again now, be surprised at the amount of jingling-worded prophecies that are attributed to him, while the poems he had wrought at are forgotten. Certainly his present-day fame rests on the bans or blessings which he is said to have uttered. The name of Haig is made perennial on Tweedside by his couplet:—

> " Betide, betide, whate'er betide,
> Haig shall be Haig of Bemersyde."

We well know that prophecies bring about their own fulfilment. There were none but spinsters in Bemersyde last century, and it seemed as if the Rhymer's ivy-mantled remnant of home would have new neighbours, but the truth-speaking prescient Thomas's words had eternally fortified the name of Haig along with the possession of Bemersyde. The ladies who had near of kin on the spindle side, sought and found a branch of the family who bore the name of Haig and to them left the old Peel. True Thomas gave voice to many malisons and desolating prophecies. He put a " gowk whate'er befa' " in a neighbouring hall to Bemersyde, and in regard to his own home at Erceldoune he said:—

"The hare shall kittle on the hearth stane,
And there never will be a Laird of Learmont again."

He made many historic forecasts, having foreseen the battles of Bannockburn, Prestonpans, and Pinkie. Of the former he said:—

"The burn of Bried
Sall run fu' reid;"

and again of the later fights between Seton and the sea:—

"Mony a man shall die that day."

According to a ballad, Thomas anticipated a bloodless victory for Scotland over her bitter foe. Brave Dunbar asked the seer—

"What man shall rule the isle Britain,
Even from the North to the Southern sea?"

He replied:—

"A French Queen shall bear the son,
Shall rule all Britain from sea to sea.
He of the Bruce's blood shall come,
As near as the ninth degree.

The waters worship shall his race,
Likewise the waves of the farthest sea;
For they shall ride over the ocean wide,
With hempen bridles and horse of tree."

So it came to pass. Mary, Queen of Scots, who was also Queen of France, bore that son, and his representative was recently, from pier and shore of Leith declared to be not only King of Great Britain and Ireland, Emperor of India, but ruler also of the British Dominions beyond the seas.

Thomas the Rhymer, perhaps depressed with the sad mechanic exercise of verse-making, seems by his prognostications to have felt his native land had much war and sorrow to wade through before "our auld enemies" the English became Scotsmen's peaceful fellow-subjects. He mentioned on what day such a storm would burst on Scotland that the effects thereof would last for generations. The day dawned fair, but before midnight the false step of a horse on the brow of a cliff at Kinghorn changed the course of our nation's history. Scotland tasted to the dregs of that cup of bitterness Solomon speaks of, "Woe to thee, O land, when thy king is a child." The hapless Stuarts succeeded one another with fated swiftness. None of the gallant Jameses lived beyond the earliest chapter of middle age, and each left for their successor a child. Alexander the Third's granddaughter and heiress was the Maid of Norroway. Sir Michael Scott had been one of the ambassadors chosen to sail to Norroway to bring the little

Margaret, the future Queen of Scots, to her motherland. She sickened on the voyage and died in Orkney. It needed no occult power to foresee, as did Michael the Wizard, gazing on the dead face of the eight-year-old princess, that dark and troubled days were in store for Scotland. Alexander III. was old, and as his descendants were gone before him when his horse fatally stumbled and left his realm kingless, the storm burst on unruled Scotland with full fury.

Prophecies are usually couched in ambiguous language, such as Thomas saying that "the teeth of the sheep shall lay the plough on the shelf." Sure enough they did, and another four-footed people, the deer, whom the chiefs have fostered for sake of sport and money have ousted the befleeced flocks from the hills. Folk lore has it that Thomas the Rhymer never died but sleeps in the Eildons, and that the hour will bring forth the man. Since his disappearance from the earth he has steadily collected horses and men. He and they will awake from slumber and come forth to aid his country in its direst need, when foes invade our shores. Arthurian legends cling to the grassy sides of the triple-headed Eildons. Merlin is said to rest there too.

There is a spot called Merlin's grave beside a thorn by the Pawsail close to the kirkyard of Drumelzier. This Merlin, Sir Thomas Dick Lauder suggests, might be some local soothsayer skilled in magic, to whom the name of the Welsh wizard was given. A well-known prognostication attributed to True Thomas says:—

> "When Tweed and Pawsail meet at Merlin's grave,
> Scotland and England shall one Monarch have."

An unprecedented flood took place on the day James VI. was crowned at Westminster, and the Tweed overflowed and met the smaller stream sure enough by Merlin's grave. Many of Thomas's prophecies have yet to be realised; one of a bloody battle on an "after day" when a three-thumbed wight shall hold three kings' horses, and where for three days, three streamlets shall run red with the blood from those who fall therein. Near by Threeburn Grange in Berwickshire a child was born at Coldingham with three thumbs, and as Napoleon then shadowed the land with fear of invasion, it was believed the holder of the kings' horses had come, and the "bloody fray" would follow.

There was a wizard who dwelt at Yester,

Adam de Gifford, about the thirteenth century. A gift of his made by his magic unperishable, still remains to testify to his powers. A neighbouring youth, a Broun of Coalstoun, courted his daughter. The lover sought his future father-in-law to inquire into his bride's dower. He found the old gentleman ruminating in his garden. The "braw wooer," hoping doubtless for a farm which lay temptingly near to his own property, broached the subject. Adam Gifford paused in his meditative stroll and pulled a pear. "This," he said, "is my daughter's dower. As long as it is preserved your lands, which will go to her descendants, will remain intact." Young Coalstoun had to be content with his economically-dowered lass. Centuries later an inquisitive bride of the Brouns tried to bite a piece out of the patriarchal pear to see how it tasted. She left marks of her teeth on the fruity heirloom, and soon after a bit of land had to be sold, so the magician's now mummified dower was placed for safe keeping in the bank, and there this Methuselah among fruits remains to-day. These wizards mentioned were all men of property and influence whose scholarship and wisdom made them all the more notable in the dark ages of ignorance, so their untutored neighbours surrounded them with a halo of mystery.

Poorer-born warlocks, seers and witches fared badly at the hands of a populace fearful of magic. The gipsies, the reputed wandering tribe from Egypt, have been famed since they came from out the East for their occult powers. Their women could give warning of coming evil or call down malisons at will. Scott drew his Meg Merrilies from authentic tales. Gipsies were ever useful in fact and fiction for their supernatural knowledge, their craftiness, their beguilements. No feat of daring was too hard for them to attempt and to accomplish. Gipsies had an inherited art of glamour. The Countess of Cassilis, who was a daughter of the Earl of Haddington, when her gipsy lover Faa and his comrades came to the gates of the earl's castle by the Doon and sang "sae sweetly," came tripping down the stairs, and they "cuist the glaumourie owre her." So she left her three bairns and her earl and went off with Johnny Faa, but he and his band were caught and "fifteen well-faured men" hung on the dule tree at the castle door. The "one fair wanton lady" whom they had lured forth was imprisoned till the end of her wrecked life in Maybole, whose walls during her long confinement, when Charles I. was king, she covered with tapestry. It was mostly the gipsy women with their supposed knowledge of palmistry that brought them within the reach of law and under the ban of witchcraft. There was a very wonderful warlock, an uneducated man gifted with second sight whose prophecies north of Tay rival True Thomas's. He is known as the Brahan Seer. This Kenneth Mackenzie divined what was to be in a pebble his mother bequeathed to him, having received it from a dead Norse princess who was buried in Scotland. When the graves gave up their dead for an hour at midnight she had far to journey overseas to revisit her native land. Mrs. Mackenzie, watching her flocks one night, saw the emptied kirkyard refill, but the one who came in the track of the Norland wind was delayed, and being a brave woman, Kenneth's mother laid the staff, which she had been herding the cattle with, across the grave. The spirit could not enter, and desired the woman to remove the hindering stick, promising her as a reward a stone for her son Kenneth in which the future would be reflected. She told his mother, how she, a daughter of the King of Norway, was drowned while bathing, and that her body had drifted to Scottish shores and was there buried. It was thus, so tradition avers, that Kenneth Mackenzie, who lived in the seventeenth century, became possessed of the stone which gave him the power of divination. He was only a day labourer, but he was sought after by the gentry throughout the length and breadth of the land, and no special assembly was complete unless the shrewd-witted Kenneth was there. He foresaw ships, full-rigged, sailing eastward and westward through the land, or as another Gaelic version of the coming Caledonian Canal puts it, " The day will come when English mares with hempen bridles shall be led round the back of Tomna-hurich." A gentleman who was writing down the seer's prophecies, when he gave tongue to this, flung them all in the fire, as he deemed this was too absurd. " The day will come when the hills of Ross will be strewed with ribbons," Kenneth had told him, and any one of us who has climbed an eminence in the Highlands and looked down sees below the Brahan Seer's " ribbons," the white roads among the heather.

He also foretold that a white house would be on every hillock, and schools and shooting lodges verify this statement. "Big sheep," vowed Mackenzie, "will overrun the country until they strike the Northern Sea," and whether it is deer or improved flocks he meant we wot not, for we have driven the clansman from his "lone shieling on the misty isle" to seek new homes in the British Dominions over the ocean. The humble seer, Kenneth, was doomed to die a cruel death. He was at a gathering at Brahan Castle, and infuriated by his keen insight in regard to those present Lady Seaforth ordered him to be seized. He fled, and before his capture he prophesied ill of the Seaforths and then flung his magic pebble into a cow's footprint, where it disappeared. He was hurried off there and then and burned in a tar barrel, and his curses came home to roost.

Dumb and deaf people seemed to be dowered with a knowledge of impending events. Many tales are told up to recent times how some sense-deprived "warlock" saw the shroud creeping up on one present or saw three women standing beside a man and enlightened him as to the names of his future spouses. These foreseers, like Kenneth Mackenzie, even as they are now, were sought for by those who are anxiously inquisitive to lift the veil from what is to come. Dante, in his *Vision of Hell, Purgatory and Paradise* represents those who on earth pretended to foretell the future going along weeping with their faces turned backwards for evermore as a punishment for their presumption in looking ahead. Among those so condemned was the "lean of flank" Michael Scott of Balwearie. But as a rule, those who divined what was to come to pass seldom fell under the ban of the law for their uncanny presages. But those who were suspected of witchcraft had a grim time of it, especially under the rule of James VI. Helpless old crones, with that economical housemate, a cat (for its foraging propensities made it independent of bite and sup) for their only companion, were credited with being in league with the powers of darkness. If the aged bodies' knowledge of the world, gained through their long pilgrimage therein, led them to hint that they knew aught beyond ordinary ken, woe betide the soothsayers. Maybe. an old wife would remark a sick child would not recover, a marriage turn out ill, and their words were remembered. A man is either a fool or a physician at forty, the proverb says, and lifelong experience had taught many an ancient, solitary dame how to cure sickness by concocting medicines from the herbs around. These " simples " were as a rule innocuous or healing, but when they failed and the patient grew worse the prescribing sybil paid a deadly debt. Two witches, in 1576, who suffered for their skill in doctoring, said they were instructed by spirits what to order. Bessie Dunlop lived in Dalry, Ayrshire, in the sixteenth century. She said the spirit of a Thomas Reid, who had tried to lure her to Elfinland, told her of herbal medicines, with which she healed many. The same was the case with Alison Pearson, who lived about the same period, and whose cousin was truly her spiritual adviser, one William Sympson. These two supernaturally-inspired doctoring women do not seem to have killed the twelve which an able medical man to-day says every student who takes an M.D. degree on an average does extinguish in his novitiate, either by stupidity or over-zeal. We speak of the credulousness and ignorance of the Middle Ages, but there are more things in earth and heaven than are dreamt of in our philosophy, and now in the twentieth century spiritualists, as they are now called, prescribe for ailments in that hub of the universe, London. They say they are directed by doctors who have gone hence but thirst to continue their healing art in this sphere. Their agent practises safely now in our Edwardian era, but gruesomely painful deaths befell the women who attempted to do so in Elizabeth's or James's time. An infirm crone, bent with age, hobbling along to her solitary hearth, mumbling to herself as she, staff in hand, stopped to peer at some passer-by, was noted. It was seen how her cat (*probably* some forlorn waif) greeted her return home. An inquisitive wayfarer looking into her cottage would spy her crouching over her fire talking to the incriminating black grimalkin. Some impudent teasing lads and lasses who had followed her she would turn on some day, exasperated by their stones and jibes. If one of these fell ill, the poor old body was seized and sentenced. According to popular credence cats and hares and witches consorted together. There was never a lack of people to swear they saw the woman change into a hare which scudded across a field. Witnesses against them were often children, seemingly devil possessed.

In Victoria's reign, to show how belief in witches still dwelt in Scotland (and this is but one authentic illustration among many), a woman was out early one morning. So was a farmer. He fired at what he thought was a hare which was making its way over a field and lamed it. Pursuing it, it disappeared, and he found the woman busy on the other side of the hedge bandaging her leg. Being entreated he promised not to tell, and she went ever after on a crutch, and he firmly believed he had shot her. This same woman cursed a boy who called her names. He died within the year, and she should have rejoiced she did not live in a century earlier, for her sentence would have assuredly been *convicta et combusta*. To catch a witch, to keep her from escaping from her own room or prevent her flying down some one else's chimney, divots of grass full of nails were placed on the chimney-tops, and this was done very recently. In past times the persecution, the torture, and the cruel death of those suspected of witchcraft forms a sorry and ghastly record. In the centre of Edinburgh, where now the trains speed through the gardened valley, the witches were tried and drowned in a pool in the then Nor' Loch. An old tree on the water edge was lately cut down, and in its wooden heart were found nails and an iron ring to which hags awaiting trial had been fastened. If they floated (and their hooped petticoats buoyed them up) they were decreed to be guilty, taken out, tortured to confess, then burned. If they sank they were thought to be innocent. Political vengeance, private spite, made many be arrested for dabbling with the forbidden craft. The Earl of Mar, brother of James III., was suspected of consulting "witches and sorcerers" so as to learn how to compass the king's end. He bled to death for this supposed conspiracy, and a dozen witches and some four warlocks were burnt at the same time to give a colour to the earl's guilt. In 1537 a Lady Glamis became a victim under a similar charge, and ladies of high degree as well as their poorer sisters were brought to trial for practising witchcraft. A Lady Foulis (*née* Katherine Ross of Balnagowan) had a step-mother's quarrel with one of her husband's, Baron Foulis, children, Robert. She was reported to have brewed poison for him, and Sir Walter Scott says Lady Foulis in 1580 was suspected of making use of "the artillery of Elf-land in order to destroy her stepson and sister-in-law." She is said to have fired fairy arrows at the pictures of her intended victims.

We need not smugly pride ourselves that we live in a less barbaric age. In John Bull's other island, not long ago, some Irish were sure a woman near them was a witch, and she was done to death. Space does not allow of us to enter into details of the lengthy death-roll of the witches. Throughout the country and in the towns the dread sentence, *convicta et combusta*, was delivered, and the populace who stood in fear of a blink from an evil eye stood by and gloated as they burned.

There were various ways of evading the curses of witches and warlocks—principally, to score the utterer "aboon the breath." My father, who was a leading light in his profession, a man in advance of his time in prophesying scientific discoveries which are yet to be, and aiding advance by tongue and pen, used to tell how his grandfather, eighteen miles from Edinburgh, angrily ordered a beggar away from his door. The beggar cursed before he departed. Alexander Simpson bethought it was bad for his homestead and crops to be under a malediction, and pursued the tramp and branded him on the forehead to annul the ban. Another method by which those who were sorcerers harmed their enemies was by making images like unto the persons they disliked. They tortured these waxen figures by piercing them with pins till their human representatives dwined and died. This superstition is referred to by Allan Ramsay in his *Gentle Shepherd*. Of Mausie, he says:—

> " Pictures oft she makes,
> Of folks she hates, and gaur expire
> Wi' slow and racking pain before the fire.
> Stuck fu' o' preens, the devilish picture melt,
> The pain by folk they represent is felt."

Some pigmy, waxen, coffined effigies were found in a niche in the stony crown of the Salisbury Crags facing Edinburgh's spires and gables. Some sorcerer had modelled these images long ago and wished the people they represented to be immured. The hair of the dog that bit you has curative powers, and it was believed if you could obtain a piece of dress from the person who ill-wished you, it would annul the evil spell. Mr. Napier, in his book of folk lore, speaks of a bride, last century, on whom the evil eye was cast. The woman suspected of malignant intent was asked to the house, and while her attention was directed elsewhere, a piece of her dress was cut off and burned, and the bride recovered. The antidote to bewitchment grows at our feet in the shape of the four-leaved clover. That is the reason we see people searching on the green carpet of grass. But in a less witch-ridden age the many-leaved clover is just thought lucky, no longer a protection from sorcery. For the benefit of those who, for good fortune's sake, hunt for this herb of grace, it might be well to quote an American's view:—

"While one will search the season over
To find the magic four-leaved clover,
Another, with not half the trouble,
Will plant a crop to bear him double."

Other modes to avoid the craft of witches lingers with us. We bang a hole in the empty egg shell, so it will not make into a boat for an evil spirit to sail in. We also put a poker up against the bars of a grate when a fire refuses to burn. The poker, so placed, with the bar of the grate, forms the all-protective cross. Witches eschewed church. As servants of the arch fiend the emblem of Christianity was gall to them, as it rendered their incantations useless. Fashionable soothsayers of to-day, along with gipsy fortune-tellers, are at times prosecuted, for, under the old statutes, presaging the future by crystal-gazing, palmistry, or tea leaves in a cup is forbidden. Fines are paid by the fashionable charlatan or imprisonment endured by the poorer gipsy clairvoyant, and the richer resume work under new mystic-sounding names. The Highlanders are still credited with a double vision of things that are yet to be and what is yet to befall. People to-day, as of yore, are as inquisitively eager to know what these gifted with this second sight may behold. Looking back from our enlightened heights we, knowing of telepathy, surmise that men like Sir Michael Scott and Thomas the Rhymer were shrewd observers, readers of human documents as well as students of Nature and her laws. Like Duke Prospero in *The Tempest* they had by knowledge acquired a potent art which reached forward to the things which were to come and which in the eyes of their contemporaries endowed them with magic power. What in their day would have been thought of a Marconi who could communicate with the ships on the ocean and send messages from land to land! Milton speaks of—

> "The airy tongues that syllable men's names
> On shores, in desert sands, and wildernesses."

And so it has come to pass. Horseless carriages seemed to be a ridiculous idea, and now through the Highlands, along the "ribbons" the poor Brahan Seer saw, they speed and boom. It is well for those who have made the forces of Nature to work for man's good, or who by study and the skill thereby obtained can use their knowledge to help scientific research, that they did not live and show their learning in the days of the first king who ruled all Britain from sea to sea. For all his boasted wisdom, his reign is marked by the bloodstains left on its annals by the war he waged against warlocks and witches.

CHAPTER VIII

FAIRS, FESTIVALS, AND FUNERALS

'Funerals and weddings and all such things as make life a delightful pageant when people go through it in large groups, dancing or mourning, but always holding hard by each others' hands."—MISS LILLY DOUGALL.

IN this restless age when people travel to and fro over the earth, when excursion tickets bridge distance even for the poor among us, we forget that in olden times a funeral, a marriage, or a christening was an occasion for a people long parted assembling together. The rarity of these meetings helped in a great measure to the hereditary ceremonies appertaining to these gatherings being stringently adhered to. The reformation which put an end to much merry-making as popish could not altogether eradicate dancing and music from the more jovial of these meetings. Stern, however, were the decrees of its ministers. In some Scottish reminiscences lately published, the author speaks of a man very recently dead, who was master of a violin and describes how attached he was to its dulcet notes. The minister pointed to him from the pulpit and said: "Thou art there behind the door, thou miserable man with the grey hair, playing thine old fiddle with the cold hand without and the devil's fire within." His family implored him to burn this violin made by a pupil of Stradivarius. The instrument with the sweet tone was sold for ten shillings, and the aged, bereft musician told how it grieved him so sorely to part with it—told how in his youth he had given the best cow in the byre for the coveted fiddle—how it spoke to him and how he loved it. He never had heart for aught again after he thus was forced to sell his friend. A minister in a neighbouring isle related how, on religious grounds, he had broken the only fiddle in his parish.

The people, despite preachers' admonitions, would not give up melody and dancing—indeed, they held to the ways of their fathers the more rigidly when conviviality was part of it, and not all the stern denunciations of the Reformation made the music mute. Rustic merry-makings could not be suppressed. There was Candlemas in the spring, Baal's fire in midsummer, much music and dancing at the kirnings held when the harvest was under thatch and rope, and on the heels of the rejoicings over garnering summer's green into sheaves, came the eerie, cheery festival of Hallowe'en. These feasts brought the people together, and they exchanged the gossip of their parishes. News travelled surely, if slowly, in the times before newspapers. However remote or isolated a neighbourhood might be, information siltered there by means of those who paid house-to-house visitations in a leisurely age. The beggars portioned themselves out districts sure of a dole from hut or hall. These mendicants were not drawn from the unemployable class, who, able-bodied and idle, are a menace on the by-roads, and to the unprotected cottager to-day. It was a simpler, kindlier age than this, and the vagrants of yore were the maimed or those enfeebled by years. They were wellnigh sure of a " piece " from every door at which they knocked. Like the monks of Buddha in Burmah, with their wallet in place of the yellow-robed priests' bowl, they afforded every one a chance to give or share with the needy and be accordingly blessed for their liberality. There is no household in Burmah but can spare some rice—

no Scottish cottage but could contribute a bit of oaten cake, for, says Henry Hall Fielding, who has laid bare *The Soul of a People*, "think not a great gift is more acceptable than a little one. You must judge by the giver's heart." Beside the beggars who circulated news from cottage and castle, there were also the scalds and bards who brought tidings as well as music with them. These musical strollers earned their food and a seat by the inglenook with the song history they told. They had for generations kept a chronicle of the events that affected our ancestors and our country. They told of deeds of war, of love, of revenge. "Inconsequent, fascinating, high-handed, impossible, picturesque, these old ballads have come to us from the childhood of the world and still speak to the child heart in us all," writes an American authoress, prefacing some of these versified annals of this island's story. The minstrel infirm and old, or the boy harper, doled out anecdotes of romance and reality which stirred the countryside as well as their repertoire of ballad chronicles. Towns could not easily as now be reached for shopping, so also tradesfolk in search of custom travelled. There was a tailor who, however many wardrobes he had to fashion or mend, had at command a new story to narrate every day. This limber-lipped man was always in request from the art he had cultivated of embroidering a plain tale. These stories told by the itinerant workmen beguiled the hours of toil, and the country customers flocked to help and hearken. Not only was it the tailors and weavers who fashioned and made up the homespun woollen garments who sought work, or bootmakers, but craftsmen, whose skilful hands could shape brooches and rings and other decorations, went around seeking occupation. When a wedding was spoken of, or a christening, and gifts were wanted, they appeared. In Perthshire there was a special family whose well-designed brooches, inlaid by some peculiar method, cannot be reproduced by the artificers of to-day with all their skill and finished tools. The cunning of the art is lost except by one family in the North of Russia, which suggests that the Scotsmen who executed this work had learned it, or inherited the knowledge from some common foreign ancestry. Scotland had from primordial times been famed for its knack of inlaying and shaping of metals into ornaments. The bracelets the Picts left in their "brochs" are specimens of this to testify to their skill, and the Romans learned from these savage inhabitants of our northland some of their methods of work. In the Middle Ages we can imagine what tales these travelling workmen would carry from one merry-making to another—tales of the gifts given to bride or babe. Then again the tailors and weavers would describe the funeral clothes they fashioned, and perhaps hint that for all the symbols of woe my lady ordered she would be taking, when a bare year had fled, another mate, and the jewellers would be sent for to fashion brooches for her delight. Every vague rumour of coming festivity, every detail of the glad or sad gathering was conned over in these newspaperless days, so beggars and bards were sure of a welcome, and in exchange for food and firelight retailed hearsay.

Funerals and feasts seem to us a curious combination, especially when we have shorn weddings of their "breakfast," and in lieu have but "a cake and wine" banquet, but in the era before railways, when roads were so rough and wheeled carriages were few, when people gathered together there was much brewing and baking for the entertainment of friends, whether the occasion of meeting was for funeral or marriage. "Whaur hae ye been, ye drunken auld deevil," a Scotsman was asked by his better half, and he replied: "I'm no sure if it was a wedding or a burial, but it was a right fine affair." The comings and the goings from this world were alike marked by feasting and drinking. To ward off the machinations of the fairies, when a babe was born the mother was never left alone till able to guard her child herself. It was thought well that the first time the child left the room it should go upstairs. Where no stairs were available the nurse ascended a ladder or a chair. On a baby's initial walk there were cakes carried and given from the infant to the first person encountered. Augury was drawn as to the infant's future by the manner in which the bairn's bread offering was received, and it was well for the child when its "first foot" turned and walked a few steps back with the nursling or blessed the babe. In the folk tales we read how at christenings fairies bad and good came to ban or endow the child. In the Borders, where the coming man had to live by raiding and fighting, his right hand was exempt from baptism, so, unhampered by Christian forbearance, he might, with unhallowed ferocity when he wished, revenge his losses. His cradle lullaby was a song, the accompaniment to which suggested the ring of foraying hoofs, for the mother in the Borderland, while she rocked her child with his unbaptised hand, crooned of his future. "If ye live ye'll steal a naggie," she assured him as she called down blessing on his downy pate. She pictured to him how he would—

> "Ride the country through and through,
> And bring hame mony a Carlisle coo;
> Through the Lowdens o'er the border,
> Weel, my baby, may ye further,
> Harry the loons of the low countree,
> Syne to the border hame to me."

Thus the mosstrooper's boy grew up imbued with the idea that his life's work was to acquire neighbouring cattle and to fight his way home from bloody forays. When in course of time he settled down with a wife, hostages to fortune only made him all the more anxious to add to his store, so when the Michaelmas moon shone mellow, with his eye upon "liftable kine"—

> "He buckled the bridle on sorrel or grey,
> Set foot to the stirrup, and up and away."

He heartened his comrades with the assurance

that " every fat steer on the haughs of the Rule shall be dower for a daughter you've left on the Tweed."

The unbaptised hand spared not any antagonistic man, or left a marketable beast in a byre on the wrong side of the marches. If by some mischance he died in his bed, great were the preparations made to prepare the funeral-baked meats, whether the rover lived in peel, tower, or farm. Mourning used, indeed, to use a Scotticism, be veritably " the Blacks." The Highlander wore his insignia of sorrow on his sleeve, as he could not alter his uniform of tartan. In the lowlands, when there was " dule and woe on the Border," not only did the rich and well-to-do families when bereft drape themselves in the garb of sorrow, but the very hangings of the furniture were also swathed in jetty darkness. In inventories of a few centuries ago " ane blake bed " was a certain part of the furnishings of a well-to-do house, and its coverlet was also of pitchy hue. In some memoirs recently published, it was mentioned that a young widow—a lass still in her teens—had been so indecorous as to complain of the sombre coverlet and hangings of the four-poster in her room, and she shocked her late husband's relatives when she begged she might at least have a white counterpane.

If a man died not by the will of God but by the hand of man, it was firmly believed that the corpse bled if touched by the person who had done the deed. When murder was suspected, each neighbour as they came to the burial put his finger on the dead man, and so strongly was this test believed in that there are many cases recorded in which people have been summoned to stand their trial because of the dead thus bearing witness, and the fact was used as evidence against them.

We all know the *Heart of Midlothian* and its heroine, Effie Deans. Her prototype was a west country lass, Isobel Walker. A flood on the river Cluden three days before Hallowe'en left on a sandbank the body of a dead child. Suppositions pointed to the fact that this gruesome piece of jetsom was the baby of the unfortunate Isobel. It was laid on her knee to see if it would reveal the tale of its brief life and bleed at her touch. It is a painfully grim picture this of the young, guilty girl and the unwelcome child she had strangled and thrown into the river, face to face once more.

With the Protestant era the Catholic manner of watching the corpse till burial did not become, as a rule, obsolete. Neighbours were always ready to sit by the dead when relatives were weary, and this usage resulted in the fostering of many superstitions and ghostly stories. All domestic animals were put out of the house on a death occurring, for it was believed if a dog or cat leapt over the corpse it might absorb his spirit and become an uncanny companion to the living, a drawback to the ascension of the soul of the dead. The mirror in the room was covered, the clock stopped and a plate of salt laid on the breast, ostensibly to prevent the body swelling, but oftener as a preventive against the devil disturbing the unburied. In some districts sin-eaters came and ate the plate of salt and of bread placed on the corpse, and so relieved the dead of sins which were hovering round, retarding the spirit from reaching the higher plane. Omens were drawn as to coming deaths from the manner the funeral party left the house, whether they straggled or walked all too quickly. It was long believed the spirit of the last person buried in a churchyard had to wait there to guard against unchristened babes or suicides being laid in the

"God's acre." Friends, to save their dead being the one thus ordained to watch the consecrated precincts, when there were to be two funerals on one day, made an unseemly rush to be first, leaving no time for the party to add stones to the cairns where the coffin rested on its last journey. A bride's first duty when she settled in her new home was to spin her own and her gudeman's grave-clothes—a fashion which brought vividly before her the fact that amid diversions and rejoicings it was well to be prepared for the inevitable end.

Of course there were a heap of traditionary usages lingering and surrounding a wedding. The bride studied the weather, anxious for fair skies and sunshine, for they were held to be tokens of happiness. She feared when cooking her last meal in her old home lest a clot of soot should fall, for that foretold ill, and cautiously she dried the dishes on her marriage morning, for if she broke one it also was a bad augury. In the brave days of old, ladies married when their parents bade them. It not unfrequently happened that many a lover knew the lass preferred him to the one chosen by father or mother, so they copied Jock o' Hazeldean, or Ronald

Macdonald who persuaded Leezie Lindsay to kilt her coats of green satin and fly with him to the Highlands. A rejected but adventuring swain who had trusty men and horses at his back could waylay the party and carry off the bride, like Lochinvar, ere the church was reached. The bride's mother, waiting at home to receive the newly-married pair on their return, in these times of bold riders was never sure who her son-in-law was till the knot was tied. Thus it became a habit for the fleet of foot among the grooms-men to race from the church and tell the news. This was called " running the brooze or braise." The rewarding brose became whisky wherewith the swift runner or rider returned, proud of his prowess, to toast as " first foot " the arriving procession. According to a custom which the Romans taught us, the bride was lifted over the threshold of her new home, and over her head was broken a cake. On fragments of this cake the bridesmaids dreamed of their coming help-mate. The tongs and poker used to be handed to the bride as a symbol she was to keep the hearth aglow. In Berwickshire, especially by the coast where the fishermen keep in a conservative manner to inherited use and wont, they "creel" the bridegroom. As he enters his house with his new-made wife a creel heavily weighted is bound on to his shoulders in such a manner he cannot rid himself of it. His friends add to his burden by heaping it with more stones till he is staggering with the weight. Then a knife is given to his wife and she, amid cheers, relieves him of his cumbersome load. This is emblematic of the assistance that a true help-mate renders and a readiness to share one another's burdens in their way through life.

Scotland was famed for and fled to by eloping pairs because of the easygoingness of its laws in regard to marriage. A simple declaration before a witness bound a couple in the bonds of matrimony as securely as red tape did in England. A blacksmith was as efficient as a minister. The disregard of the church as the place to make their vows in may have arisen in Scotland from a unique usage called handfasting, or hand in the fist marriages. This vogue arose in early Catholic times when travelling was dangerous and difficult, and visits from priests in outlying districts rare. A fair was held annually in the dale where the Black and White Esk met, and there flocked the unmarried of both sexes who sought a companion. When they found one to their mind they were handfasted till the following year. Then if they mutually approved of one another, a priest in course of time when he came by gave them the Church's blessing. These peripatetic monks were called "book-in-the-bosom" priests, as they carried a breviary and a rough register in their robes of approved and church-sanctioned handfasters. This "on trial" marriage system seems to have been the fashion with ladies of high degree as well as with the Eskdale lasses and lads. Lindsay says "That James, sixth Earl of Murray, had a son by Isabel Innes, daughter of the Laird of Innes, Alexander Dunbar, a man of singular wit and courage. This Isabel was but handfasted to him and deceased before the marriage." Mr. Guthrie, in *Old Scottish Customs*, says, "If either of the parties insisted on a separation and a child was born during the year of trial, it was to be taken care of by the father only, and to be ranked among his lawful children next after his heirs. The offspring was not treated as illegitimate, because the custom was justified being such and instituted with a view of making way for a happy, peaceful marriage. Such was also the power of custom, that the apprenticeship for matrimony brought no reproach on the separated lady, and if her character was good she was entitled to an equal match as though nothing had happened." It is said that a desperate feud ensued between the clans Macdonald of Sleat and Macleod of Dunvegan, owing to the former chief having availed himself of this licence to send back the sister or daughter of the latter. Macleod resenting the indignity observed, "That since there was no wedding bonfire there should be one to solemnise the divorce," and he accordingly laid waste to the territories of the Macdonalds, and they kindled "sic a lowe" cottages and strong castles were "smoored in the dark reek." Gretna Green on the south border, Lamberton Toll three miles north of Tweed, just without the boundary of the changeable town of Berwick, and Coldstream, were raced to by eloping couples, and hard by the toll bar in each case dwelt a blacksmith. His legitimate work of shoeing horses kept him on the spot, so the mighty man of the hammer and forge became the recipient of the elopers' declaration. The registers of the Lamberton Toll runaway marriages were sent to the county town of Greenlaw, but as

"Duns dings a'" and it has now succeeded Greenlaw, there the registers abide, records of hasty marriages of long ago suggesting flight and followers, and often doubtless there was repentance at leisure, in many cases life-long repentance as the days of handfasting were over.

Fairs of all kinds were the centre of meetings and merry-makings. In the Borders also there were the Riding of the Marches to declare the free rights of the town, such as the Common Riding at Hawick, Selkirk, the boundaries of Berwick, etc. These ridings, on a specified day, are still extant, shorn of their former glory but even now maintained to uphold the peculiar tenures and charters of liberty attached to the ceremony; and we see paragraphs from time to time in the evening papers telling of them, with bands and flags and holiday sightseers. The border Scots were fond of sports, with the results that many an unpremeditated feud followed on the heels of some peaceful gathering for games. Boasts as to their prowess led to wagers or jealousies, and the gauntlet was thrown down. The "stout Erle of Northumberland" vowed he'd "ding the dun deer down" on Scottish soil, and went forth with his train to what proved to be the " woeful hunting " of Chevy Chase, where a Percy and a Douglas died, and of twenty hundred Scottish spears scarce " fifty-five did fly," and of fifteen hundred English men went home but fifty-three—

> " The rest in Chevey Chase were slaine,
> Under the greenwood tree."

Many another hunt with bows and arrows handy led to fierce frays. Even a football match, with the victors triumphant, the losers sore at heart, was a pretext for mischief being brewed and feuds fought to the death, as in the case of the warden of the Middle Marches in 1600, one Sir John Carmichael, who was murdered on returning from a football match. Under the guise of a ba' playing the men mustered in strength, and when the play was played they indulged in a raid over the border. In the ballad of the Bonnie Earl of Moray he not only tilted at the glove, but " he played at the ba' " and whether that ba' belonged to golf, rackets, or football, we know not. Likely enough he who " was fit to be a king " was good at all three. Scotland is the cradle of the most popular of ball games—golf—which, like the thistle that it also reared, has taken root and spread over the world.

Golf was played on Scottish links before Columbus discovered America, and statutes were made when the centuries were barely in their teens in regard to the "royal game," to stem its popularity, for men were more keen in contesting a match with club and ball than learning to aim swift and sure with weapons of war. The links lured the men from practising at the bow butts, and the law insisted that whether the Scots were soldiers of the king or not, they were to be ready, aye ready, to withstand against their auld enemies the English. There were wapenshaws regularly held. This show of weapons was to prove that the implements of death were in order and the men competent to wield them. Edinburgh as the capital took the lead. It had a blue blanket for a banner, which was the first to flutter over volunteers. When it was waved shopkeepers, artificers, and craftsmen had to lay down the yard measure, the hammer and tools of trade, and swarm forth equipped at a moment's notice to man the walls and bend the bow. Such good service did these counter-jumpers and workmen do that James III. gave them a new blue banner; but the old one is still extant to show how Edinburgh merchantmen were a well-trained volunteer band, trained in times of peace and ready to rally around their provost or convener. Tradition says this standard was originally unfurled in the cause of the Holy Wars by a crusading body of citizens of Edinburgh, and that their blue banner was the first to be planted on the walls of Jerusalem when that city was stormed by the Christian army under the famous Godfrey de Bouillon. James III., having been held captive by his rebellious nobles for nine months in the Castle of Edinburgh, was freed by the citizens of "High Dunedin," who raised the Blue Blanket, assaulted, surprised, and captured the castle. Out of gratitude for their seasonable loyalty the king, besides granting them certain privileges, presented them with a new ensign of blue silk, with authority to display the same in defence of their king, country, and their own rights when these were assailed. To keep these volunteers who mustered under the Blue Blanket in shooting trim, golf and other games of "ba'" were only permitted after a stipulated amount of archery had been practised.

The love of football is still strong in rural districts. In the village of Coldingham in Berwickshire there used to be an annual match played on the moor, bachelors *versus* the married men. A hole in the earth was the benedicts' boundary, and latterly a barn door of a farm erected on the site was aimed at by them instead. At a neighbouring village of Foulden a football match was played on Fasten' E'en between the men of the village and their neighbouring county men. The goals were a mill happer and the pulpit of the kirk.

Another Scottish game which has gone overseas to the Great Lone land is curling. It is a social game. The laird and the mason frozen out of work meet on the rink on a level. The skip is the best man, be he earl or convicted poacher. Curling has so much of a language of its own and that broad Scotch, it is not likely to be so cosmopolitan a game as "gowff."

Old ways rooted on some fact or olden usage linger on indelible. The children of St. Andrews had a game peculiar to their grey city by the sea, which they played, singing to it a rhyme which told its origin—

> "Marry, maidens, marry, maidens, marry, maidens, now,
> For stickit is your cardnal and sauted like a sow."

Thus in this jingle is recalled the murder of Cardinal Beaton—his body was preserved in salt by the conspirators during the time they held the castle against the government forces. Children are conservative in their games and in their unshakable preference for rhymes and plays whose origin is traceable to some historic event, or lost in the mist of fable. Generations of boys and girls through the centuries have danced and sung to the old rune, King and Queen of Cantelon.

"How many miles to Babylon?" children in pairs ask, and two others as gate-keepers whose arms bar the way reply, "Three score and ten."

"Will we get there by candlelight?" ask the would-be travellers.

"Yes and back again," assert those who act as toll-keepers.

"Open your gates and let us through," command the intending voyagers; but this peremptory order is not obeyed. The young rovers must be polite, for they are forbidden to proceed until they "beck or bow," and so the expectant pilgrims curtsey and bow.

"There's a beck—and there's a boo," they cry, "open your gates and let us through," and they gaily are off to visit the king and queen, and reach Babylon, for the small explorers all of an afternoon are many of "the thousand things that children are" to reach the East and be back by candlelight is quite an easy feat for the quick-witted small people.

One who did not forget his childhood or the old refrain, speaking of such expeditions says—

> "Our phantom voices haunt the air
> As we were still at play,
> And I say hear them call and say,
> How far is it to Babylon?
> On we rode, the others and I,
> Over the mountains blue and high!
> A thousand miles we galloped fast,
> And down the witches' lane we passed,
> And from our steeds alighted down
> Before the gates of Babylon."

The well-known lilt and its words come back after we have wandered many a weary foot in life's journey. With a rush of recollection of the golden days of childhood we hear the youngsters inquiring the way to the ancient city. Who the King and Queen of Cantelon were no one stops to ask. Children from age to age go off to visit them singing the same words and the same melody—they like them for old sake's sake. That has been one of the rhyming tales that has come down from the dim pagan past for ever, like Merry-ma-tanzie, to tinkle in our memories. We know from whence sprang—

> "Willie, Willie Wastle,
> Stand on my castle;
> And a' the dogs o' your town
> Will no drive Willie Wastle down."

On sandhill, or hearthrug doing duty for a mound, a boy awaits the attack of the others on his castle, and fine sport invaders and defiant custodian have till Willie Willie Wastle is hurled from his castle. This "game" began in the big game of war—no child-play—when in 1651 one John Cockburn was governor of the Castle of Hume on its high knoll, and refused to yield to Cromwell. The defiant words children sing when in possession, the original Willie Willie Wastle wrote in reply to the order of the king-killer so austerely championing freedom, to surrender, but alack! a breach by the Ironsides' artillery was made in the wall, and Cockburn was dinged down. Little do the lads and lasses think with what a sore heart John Cockburn, the author of Willie Wastle, stepped from his high-seated castle, which overlooked such a fertile track of country.

Curious remnants of plays have come down to us in the children's perennial runes. Strange fragments of folk song the little people have thus preserved like Janet Jo, which is still sung by children in city alley or village street. Janet Jo, whose lover comes to " court " her, saw him not. Her parents turn him away as she was washing. When he returns she is always bleaching, drying, etc., and then he is told " Janet Jo is dead and gone." A funeral follows and a wail for Janet Jo. It is a remnant of some mayhap " owre true tale," which laid hold of the popular imagination, and which the children treasured as you ofttimes see them treasure little bits of broken china which their seniors have cast forth, and which they have set up as the chief ornament of their play-house. No new gewgaw bought at a fashionable toyshop can oust the effete fragment from favour, and in course of time the small people's conservative taste wins the day, for their elders come to admire even the scrap of what had once been an treasured.

CHAPTER IX

ADAGES AND OMENS

> " From the barred visor of Antiquity,
> Reflected shines the eternal light of Truth
> As from a mirror. . . .
> Even thus transformed,
> Rude popular traditions and old tales
> Shine as immortal poems."
>
> LONGFELLOW.

THOUGH the origin of many of our everyday uses and wonts are hidden in the well of years, some still float on the surface, for it is odd how certain scraps of folk lore take deep root in the popular fancy and never die out. " God bless you," we say when a friend sneezes. According to Sir Frederick Treves, sneezing repels the invading microbes of cold. Long ago in Greece, when the plague was prevalent, the threatened victims at the crisis of the disease averted the fatal catastrophe by allowing nature's artillery of sneezing to oust the enemy, so the benediction was spoken by friends, and that prayerful aspiration despite the flight of centuries is offered by us to-day. Wise saws in regard to weather and the gales of life are still evergreen—rhymes of people and places are indelibly printed in our minds. The Lightsome Lindsays as well as the Gordons are named in the ballad on the Battle of Otterbourne. The former flew—

> " . . . like fire about
> Till a' the fray was done."

The latter are described as the Gordons *guid*, but " gay " is the word usually applied to them. In a well-known song, of all the twenty-four nobles who sat in the king's hall, Glenlogie (prosaically George Gordon) is the " flower of them a'," and he is one of the Gay Gordons. These—the Lightsome Lindsays and Gay Gordons —flash through history in times past and present with " *gallant* Grahams," the " *gentle* Johnstons," and Setons tall and proud. A Border rhyme includes many men of the Merse:—

> " The haughty Humes,
> The saucy Scotts,
> The cappet Kers,
> The bauld Rutherfords."

There are a host of Scottish families with an alliterative or descriptive title before their names, gleaned from friends, enemies, and more often from some "sabre cut of Saxon speech," some truesome word in the ballads which has stuck to them and given them the distinctive character they are known by the world over. Some of these territorial families also own heirlooms which have come to them legend guarded. We have spoken of the Coalstoun pear, of the fairy banner of Dunvegan, and other fetiches are scattered over Scotland. For instance, there is "Barbreck's bone" in the Antiquarian Museum—an important healing relic. It is a slice of ivory, and belonged to the Barbrecks in Argyleshire. It was believed to be useful in curing insanity, and a bond of £100 was required when it was loaned. These relics were dipped in water which the patient drank. The Lee penny of the Lockharts, famed for its medicinal powers, was hired to Newcastle when in Charles the First's reign the plague was rife there, and £6000 was the money pledged for its safe return. The Robertsons of Struan had a famous stone, potent in healing, and also from time immemorial the Stewarts of Ardvoirlich had one, the "Clach Dearg." There is also the charm stone of the Bairds of Auchmeddan, in appearance more like a bone than a stone, a round putty-coloured ball.

It was said to have come from the Holy Land. It may have been some sacred bone gotten there by a crusader. Alongside this relic there is kept in a safe by a descendant of the Bairds a bear's paw. The bear, in the days of William the Lion, attacked the king, and the progenitor of the Bairds stepped forward, slew the beast, and there to this day, in Edinburgh, is treasured the dried paw of the four-footed, might-have-been regicide who disputed the right of entry to the woods with Scotland's king. Within hearing of the time gun of Edinburgh are two estates whose tenure, according to history fostered by folk lore, is simple and romantic, going back to the heroic age of Scotland's Jameses. The Clerks of Penicuik were granted their estate " free for a blast." They hold themselves bound to sit on a rock called the Buckstone and blow three times upon a horn when royalty comes to hunt upon the Borough Muir, where the troops assembled before fatal Flodden. The family who bear the motto, " Free for a Blast," are saved by builders and the encroachments of the city from ever seeing a king hunt again on what once was a moor, now a suburb crowded with flats and villas lying between the city and the Pentlands.

At Cramond Brig, five miles from Edinburgh, there is the farm of Braehead where, in James the Fifth's days, dwelt Jock Howieson, who saved the king from some gipsies and afterwards dressed his wounds. James had been masquerading as the Gudeman of Ballengeich when he fell foul of the nomads. As the kindly farmer washed his unknown guest's wounds he told him of his desire to own his farm, and the "gudeman" trysted him to meet him at Holyrood and lay his plaint before James. Here honest Jock found the stranger he had entertained (who beside his simple self, at the Court, alone wore his hat) was the king, and he was gifted with his farm on condition he, or the holders thereof, came laden with basin and towel to the sovereign of Scotland when they crossed Cramond Brig. George IV. was thus greeted by the holder of Braehead.

The Lockharts of Carnforth held their land by instituting a race at the annual fair for a pair of red hose, and when the prize was won the laird had a mounted messenger in readiness to speed with the news to the Lord Advocate.

Round places there remained a halo of ancient prophecies. Thomas the Rhymer marked many spots, and local folk lore in popular jangles marked many more. Robert Chambers tells of an old man of seventy-two, who, in 1825, told how he had heard the following prophetic couplet when a boy, and in his childhood. Remember Edinburgh then was enclosed within its ancient walls, and there was then no talk of the Lang Gait turning into Princes Street:—

> "York was, London is, and Edinburgh will be
> The biggest of the three."

There are other prognostications which were made centuries ago, and by the wear and tear of winds and waves, or the encroachments of the ocean, seem to be coming true, and on their fulfilment the prophet foretells the world is nearing its end:—

> "When the Yowes o' Gowrie come to land,
> The day of judgment's near at hand."

These stony "yowes" are close to Invergowrie —two blocks of rock which were once out in the sea. The estuary has silted up and the country people say the land gains an inch a year. On Sunday afternoon it was a custom to go to see what progress the yowes were making.

> "When Finhaven Castle runs to sand,
> The world's end is near at hand,"

says a Forfar rhyme. Once solid Finhaven is a

ruin, and it is highly probable time will crumble its remaining walls into sand.

The people of districts from song and story have been named mostly like those relating to families with an alliterative word. Berwickshire boasts of the Men of the Merse, and there are gay lads o' Gala water. The shoemakers—the Souters of Selkirk—made themselves a name, and Scotland itself, with oaten cakes and its women bakers of toothsome bread, is known the world over as the Land o' Cakes.

> " Glasgow is famed for bells,
> Lithgow for wells,
> Carrick for a man,
> Kyle for a cow,
> Cunningham for corn and bere,
> And Galloway for woo',"

are well-known rhymes specifying places.

The borrowing days of March from April are well known:—

> " March borrows frae April
> Three days and they are ill.
> The first of them is wind and weet,
> The second it is snow and sleet,
> The third of them is peel-a-bane
> And freezes the wee birds' nebs tae the stane."

There is a time-proven proverb bearing in mind March's extremes, changing as it ofttimes

P 2

does from a lion to a lamb. Whether the weather be fair or foul on St. Swithin's is to-day studied as in bygone times. If fine, it insures six weeks' spell of clear skies; if wet, rain daily. The freakish uncertainty of our climate, the deceptiveness of spring, when the sun shines gaily one day and the next may be as cold again as winter, has made wise ones warn the coming generation to—

> " Ne'er cast a clout
> Till May be out."

When snow falls, the Scotch child is told it is Norroway witches shaking their feathers; and when rain splashes down it seems to be well to advise it to go to Spain, whether in resentment, or that it is needed there, we know not.

There are many prophecies in regard to weather from local signs—hills which wear a cowl and bring rain to the plains.

> " When Falkland Hill puts on his cap,
> The Howe o'Fife will get a drap,"

say the folk of Fife, and in Annandale they have noted—

> " When Criffel wears a hap,
> Skiddaw wats full well o' that."

" Many haws, many snaws," the old folks say,

when they see the thorn white with blossom, believing that a foreseeing Providence will supply more food if a hard winter is to set in. Simple signs and portents were read often aright in what we would call unlettered days, and old-world quaint saws are still taught. The early poems of romance are full of haggard suggestions, for the songs of a younger world were oftwhiles sad songs. They held the popular imagination longer in thrall. The rattle and shallow catchiness of modern music hall verses a primitive people, burdened with the difficulty of fighting for existence, would have naught of. It is a proven fact that the saddest story ever maketh the sweetest song, and in the old ballads, where lies enshrined much folk lore, the ower-words in them has a plaintive note, but also a note so full of force it retains its hold on all those who hearken to it—

> " For every stroke goes o'er thy harp
> It *stounds my heart within.*"

Many superstitions which were credited by the people appear in the ballads. A ring bursting on the finger was held to presage evil, as in " Lammlain "—

> "The Lord sat in England,
> A-drinking the wine.
> I wish a' may be weel
> Wi' my lady at hame;
> For the rings of my fingers
> They're now burst in twain."

Hynde Horn alludes to change of colour in diamonds as betokening ill. When he returned, after being seven years at sea, he begged of his should-have-been bride in the guise of a beggar, and in the empty cup let fall the ring saying—

> "Now that the diamonds are changed in their hue,
> I know that my love has to me proved untrue."

Precious stones in the East are said to have properties which suit only with certain temperaments, and these stones belong to people born in certain months and are their lucky mascots. Opals, despite their beauty, are as a rule avoided for an engagement ring, being believed, perhaps because of their changeableness, to be unstable. Amber from ancient times is held to have special properties—lammer is the Scottish word for it. It was potent in blindness, and a charm against evil spirits. Amber necklaces were worn as a charm against evil. Betty Davidson, to whose tales Burns listened when he was a glowing-eyed boy, had a string of "lammer beads" which enabled her to speak of bogles and witches and Old Hornie himself without fear. From the protection the amber gave her, her nimble tongue had full licence to describe the ghouls she knew of, and to her we maybe owe Burns's description of the pranks of the witches in "Tam o' Shanter." In the ruins of a Pict's stronghold on a Border stream recently was found an amber bead, treasured by its owner unnumbered centuries ago, and sorely missed when it rolled away and hid itself from human sight, to be upheaved by the plough along with the elf arrows the Pict fashioned.

A picture falling or a mirror being broken are omens of ill we still attach importance to The crown tottered when placed on James II.'s head at Westminster, and a courtier had to steady it; his family, he said, had often before supported the crown. It was a portent which was noted at the time, and its prophecy was not long of fulfilment.

The Stone of Destiny is the largest "precious stone" in this country. Whether it be the one, as tradition sayeth, on which Jacob rested his head when he dreamed, and through many a weary pilgrimage was carried by his descendants as a talisman, here it was coveted, for the Lia Fail was ordained to be the throne seat of the monarch who would rule the earth. Edward I. of England bore it away, but destiny sent kings from Scotland to be crowned upon it. When Sir Walter Scott was escorting Mungo Park across the hills to Yarrow before the explorer set out on his last travels, Park's horse stumbled and nearly fell. "A bad omen," said the Shirra. "Freits (omens) follow those who look for freits," replied Park, thinking of the words of the old ballad, "Edom o' Gordon"—

> "Them look to freits, my master dear,
> Then freits will follow them."

Prophecies truly bring about their own fulfilment. Take, for instance, the case of the Haigs of Bemersyde, and looking back over ages of folk lore we may shudder, or smile, at the superstitious dread our ancestors had of what we call the forces of nature—thunder, shrieking winds, darkness, etc. They were a people dwelling in close communion with the earth and sky. Living in so austere and simple a manner they saw and heard with senses unblunted by the requirements of civilisation, sharpened indeed by their rude hand-to-hand encounter with the beasts of the forest for a livelihood. We see in all the oral traditions they left us how they believed in elves and hobgoblins, ourisks, etc. "O sweet and far from cliff and scar," says Tennyson, "the horns of Elfland faintly blowing." Instead of their musical trumpets sounding through the hills and adown the dales, we of this advanced age only hear the horns of motors coming to smother the sauntering wayfarer in dust, and frightening even the idea of fairies out of mind. This peace-loving era has tried to put Satan behind it, to banish the prince of darkness from our creed. The very names by which he was mentioned, Auld Clootie, Hornie, etc., are sinking into oblivion—names invented, while he reigned, by terror, to evade mentioning him, so that none should be heard by his emissaries "speaking ill of the deil." However, the pendulum swings. Spiritualism is now the fashion. The denizens of Elfinland, the good neighbours of old, are supposed no longer to cast their glamour over us, but as astral spirits enliven seances. Ghosts still walk and talk to some of us, but even this material age cannot deprive us of the romance that superstition and fairies have left in our minds and in the best of our literature. The old, old stories of folk lore still dwell evergreen in our memories. All the time-tried, imperishable favourites—Puss in Boots, Red Riding-hood, Cinderella (Rushie coat, in Scotland), Bluebeard, Jack and the Bean Stalk, etc.—folk lore has saved to us, showing the oneness in speech of the Teutonic races. " Amid curious rubbish you will find sound sense if you look for it. You will find the creed of the people as shown in their stories. You will find perseverance, frugality, and filial piety rewarded, pride, greed, and laziness punished. Men in this century have raised up a pastime for children, fit to be a study for the energies of grown men, to all the dignity of a science. It is held by those who have studied the subject that the stories we all know, the very games children play and the refrains they sing to them, came from the East. The problem in each case was to trace the nursery tale to the legend, and the legend to the myth, and the myth to the earliest germ, and as far as possible to indicate the foreign interpolations when they occurred, and account for the local corrections. In this way the history of a story, like the history of a word, was frequently more interesting, more instructive than the history of a campaign." So says one student of folk lore, and another that: "The record of these customs is more than a matter of antiquarian curiosity, for it may help to throw light upon the life and the literature of Scotland in bygone days, and surely everything that enables us to understand our forefathers better is to be commended and ought to be regarded as highly instructive."

Every step we take on Scottish soil we tread on history, as Cicero said men at Athens did, and also in our ears when we walk in the lowlands ring the superstitions which by traditions have come to us from the rawest beginnings of our islands' races. We treasure now all antique things, including the "ancient haunts of men." From a few bones those skilled in their study can reconstruct the type to which they belonged. So from the circle of monoliths, from antiquarian odds and ends, flint arrowheads, bronze and gold ornaments, the plough, or the pick-axe digging tunnels for railroads, brings to the light of our day, place names which speak of an obsolete people, we, who for the present are in the forefront of time, from these fragments left, surmise how our forefathers lived and worshipped. Their "distant footsteps echo through the corridors of time." We have tried, we trust not in vain, to read the cypher of their myths and remains aright. The ancient customs and beliefs of antiquity cling to us and colour our fancies. The ancientness, the romance of the unfathomed, attracts us. Some superstitions are enshrouded in a pre-historic mist, but the very doubtfulness of their outline looming in the background haunts us in the same way that an unascended mountain overshadowing an alpine climber entices and beckons him to ascend, invade, and learn the secrets of its heights and solitudes.

The unread carvings on the cromlechs, the traditions of ages past, are elements in the life of our nation which it is well to foster, if they only show us from what level we have ascended to the dignity of reasoning beings.

THE TEMPLE PRESS, PRINTERS, LETCHWORTH

www.ingramcontent.com/pod-product-compliance
Lightning Source LLC
LaVergne TN
LVHW091129080826
845145LV00008B/2090